THE GOLDEN CORD

THE

GOLDEN CORD

A SHORT BOOK ON THE SECULAR AND THE SACRED

CHARLES TALIAFERRO

University of Notre Dame Press
Notre Dame, Indiana

Library of Congress Cataloging-in-Publication Data
Taliaferro, Charles.
    The golden cord : a short book on the secular and the sacred /
Charles Taliaferro.
        pages   cm
    Includes bibliographical references and index.
    ISBN-13: 978-0-268-04238-7 (pbk. : alk. paper)
    ISBN-10: 0-268-04238-1 (pbk. : alk. paper)
    E-ISBN: 978-0-268-09377-8
    1. God (Christianity) 2. Life—Religious aspects—Christianity.
3. Self—Religious aspects—Christianity. 4. Redemption—Christianity.
5. Cambridge Platonism. I. Title.
    BT103.T35   2012
    230—dc23
                                2012037000

∞ *The paper in this book meets the guidelines for permanence and durability
of the Committee on Production Guidelines for Book Longevity
of the Council on Library Resources.*

CONTENTS

ACKNOWLEDGMENTS

I am deeply grateful for the patience, graciousness, support, and encouragement of the University of Notre Dame Press's senior editor, Charles Van Hof. For help in preparing the manuscript and for editorial comments and research, I am in debt to Tricia Little, Olivia James, Therese Cotter, Rebecca Dyer, Elisabeth Granquist, Aaron Stauffer, Matt Rohn, Alexis Anne Arnold, Sam Dunn, Andrea Ohles, Eric Erfanian, and Julia Megumi Ortner. For comments on earlier versions of this text, I am most grateful to Elsa Marty, Natasha Fredericks, Joshua and Jenna Farris, and two anonymous reviewers for the University of Notre Dame Press. I also thank Ann Aydelotte for her expert copyediting. I have learned a great deal from Jil Evans through our co-authorship of *The Image in Mind*, and I am infinitely grateful for our many exchanges on the themes of *The Golden Cord*. As always, I dedicate this work to Jil with love. It is also for The Great Conversation, a two-year course on great works of literature, philosophy, and art with Kathryn Ananda-Owens, and David Booth, for truly great conversations that surround the central themes of the book. In their company I found (as I hope all who read this may find) an extraordinarily deep and caring fellowship, in which disagreements were surrounded by an evident, ardent care for each other. At best, I suggest that Augustine's account of philosophical camaraderie is ideal:

> And friendship had other charms to captivate my heart. We could talk and laugh together and exchange small acts of kindness. We could join in the pleasure that books can give. We could be grave or gay together. If we sometimes disagreed, it was without spite, as a man might differ with himself, and the rare occasions of dispute were the very spice to season

our usual accord. Each of us had something to learn from the others and something to teach in return. If any were away, we missed them with regret and gladly welcomed them when they came home. Such things as these are heartfelt tokens of affection between friends. They are the signs to be read on the face and in the eyes, spoken by the tongue and displayed in countless acts of kindness. They can kindle a blaze to melt our hearts and weld them into one.[1]

I also must express my utmost gratitude to Mr. and Mrs. T, who were at the beginning and who impressed on me the important difference between cleverness and wisdom and the vital need to love wisdom, especially when this seems profoundly unfashionable.

Some of the arguments on naturalism, the mind-body relationship, the problem of evil, redemption, and glory have been explored in public presentations at St. Olaf College (especially the Last Lecture of 2009, 2010, and 2011), Oxford University, St. Andrews University, Washington and Lee University, Marquette University, Macalester College, Augustana College, Ursinus College, Pennsylvania State University, Indiana University, Grand Valley State University, Middlebury College, Copenhagen University, and the University of Wisconsin. I am deeply grateful for dialogues on each of these occasions. The work on redemption is seriously influenced by discussions with Paul Reasoner and by our collaboration on a manuscript on redemption. I am also indebted to Craig Lindahl-Urben for many years of conversation on the seductive nature of glory. And I gratefully acknowledge my immense debt to David Weir, a friend, wise counselor, and mentor throughout my life, who has taught me great things about the secular and the sacred.

1. *Confessions of Saint Augustine*, trans. R. S. Pine-Coffin (New York: Viking Penguin, 1961), Book 4, p. 79.

INTRODUCTION

A woman once told the author of *For Whom the Bell Tolls* and *Death in the Afternoon*, Ernest Hemingway, that she preferred stories with happy endings. Hemingway is said to have replied: "Madame, all stories, if continued far enough, end in death, and he is no true storyteller who would keep that from you."[1]

It certainly appears that Hemingway has a point. After all, as Jerry Walls points out in an otherwise cheerful book on Christian views of the afterlife, all marriages will end in death or divorce.[2] His observation may be extended: All friendships, romances, family ties, professor-student relations, author-editor-and-reader relations, business partnerships, and so on, appear to end either at death or some time before death by way of quarrels, breakups, accidents, a failure of energy or interest, and the like. Beyond our individual fate, and the ending of all our relationships in this life, it seems that our story as a species on earth is not bound for a cheerful conclusion. Modern cosmologists claim that our sun is roughly halfway through its life, and that in about 4.5 billion years the sun will have run out of hydrogen, collapse, and then (using contemporary jargon) become a "red dwarf" and then a "black dwarf." In this process the earth will be vaporized, and then what is left of our former solar system will drift along with the rest of the Milky Way on its collision course with our neighboring Andromeda galaxy. All this seems to get rather close to what Pierre

1

Teilhard de Chardin, the French Jesuit paleontologist and mystic, called "absolute death."

> Multiply to your heart's content the extent and duration of progress. Promise the earth a hundred million more years of continuous growth. If, at the end of that period, it is evident that the whole of consciousness must revert to zero, *without its secret essence being garnered anywhere at all,* then, I insist, we shall lay down our arms—and mankind will be on strike. The prospect of a *total death* (and that is a word to which we should devote much thought if we are to gauge its destructive effect on our souls) will, I warn you, when it has become part of our consciousness, immediately dry up in us the springs from which our efforts are drawn.[3]

Whether or not "total death" is as dispiriting as Teilhard de Chardin suggests, it would be the ultimate ending of the story of the cosmos from a Hemingway perspective.

This book is a response to the secular naturalism that lies behind Hemingway's conjecture and the above portrait of life's passing significance. While "naturalism" will need to be more carefully defined later, at the outset it can be taken as the thesis that nature alone exists and that there is no transcendent God, soul, or afterlife. The key thesis of naturalism is that, while you and I may be passionately committed to values, the cosmos itself is utterly impersonal and without purpose. In *The View from Nowhere*, an important book that includes a section on the meaning of life, Thomas Nagel observes that "[f]rom an external view of the universe, which abstracts from our own position in it, it . . . wouldn't have mattered if we had never existed."[4] Nagel writes eloquently about the tension between the importance we feel (from our own point of view) about our life and death and the complete indifference of the cosmos itself. "From far enough outside my birth seems accidental, my life pointless and my death insignificant, but from inside my never having been born seems nearly unimaginable, my life monstrously important, and my death catastrophic."[5] Of course, naturalists relish and profoundly value life, and even the cosmos. But, by their lights, the cosmos is not something that can or does care about its constituents. The cosmos does not itself have some kind of objective meaning or purpose, nor does it exist because it is good or valuable in itself.

The main thesis—or question—that this book addresses is whether there are signs all around us that we live in a created order and are made for something other than absolute death. I will nail my colors to the mast at the outset: I side with a form of Christianity that received a brave, extraordinary expression in a mid-seventeenth-century movement in England called Cambridge Platonism. Members of this movement—Henry More, Ralph Cudworth, Benjamin Whichcote, Peter Sterry, and John Smith among others—developed a nonmechanistic, nonmaterialistic philosophy that gave center place to the love of the good, the true, and the beautiful. They thought that we are surrounded in ordinary experience by signs of God's living, abundant reality. And they upheld this fundamentally positive view of reality amid the violence and ugly strife of the English civil war, which, while it did not involve *absolute death*, involved the death of tens of thousands.[6] The Cambridge Platonists held that at the heart of all reality is absolute life. They probably would not be at all unsettled by the current predictions of the end of life in our cosmos in contemporary cosmology. After all, the New Testament itself predicts an end of the cosmos (Matt. 24:35). But because of the New Testament faith in a God of powerful love, there is also the promise of a new cosmos (Rev. 21:1).[7]

The Cambridge Platonist view can be traced from the New Testament, especially the Johannine sources (in John 10:10, Jesus sees his life work as bringing about abundant life) through the Alexandrian Platonists Clement of Alexandria and Origen, and through the Florentine academy and the wonderful Marcilio da Ficino. In terms of popular twentieth-century Christian writers, something of Cambridge Platonist spirituality may be seen in the works of C. S. Lewis, J. R. R. Tolkien, Dorothy Sayers, and Charles Williams.[8] The contrast between Nagel's impersonal cosmic vision and the Christian Platonist position could not be clearer. While Nagel sees a severe clash between our personal, individual values and the impersonal nature of the cosmos (or life as viewed from an objective or external point of view), Cambridge Platonist Peter Sterry believes that we are invited to relish the great sea of divine love:

Dear Reader, if you would be led to that sea, which is as the gathering together, and confluence of all the waters of life, of all truths, goodness, joys, beauties, and blessedness, follow the stream of the divine love, as it holds on its course, from its head in eternity through every work of God, through every creature. So shall you be not only happy in your end, but in your way, while this stream of love shall not only be your guide by the side, but shall carry you along in its soft and delicious bosom, bearing you up in the bright arms of its divine power, sporting with you all along, washing you white as snow in its own pure floods, and bathing your whole spirit and person in heavenly inexpressible sweetness.[9]

A Dinner Party with Virginia Woolf
or a Summer Evening with W. H. Auden?

The difference between secular naturalism versus Cambridge Platonist philosophies may be compared to two evening parties. A secular naturalist-style party may be imbued with humor, friendship, romance, and more. These goods, however, are enjoyed while all that is outside the dinner party is hostile and bleak. The scene is akin to Virginia Woolf's description in *To the Lighthouse*. After a rough start, the dinner party comes to life:

> Now all the candles were lit up, and the faces on both sides of the table were brought nearer by the candlelight, and composed, as they had not been in the twilight, into a party round a table, for the night was now shut off by panes of glass, which, far from giving any accurate view of the outside world, rippled it so strangely that here, inside the room, seemed to be order and dry land; there, outside, a reflection in which things wavered and vanished, watery.
>
> Some change at once went through them all, as if this had really happened, and they were all conscious of making a party together in a hollow, on an island; had their common cause against that fluidity out there.[10]

In the secular naturalist framework, however, the party and dinner partners all pass or seem to pass (especially if memories fade) into oblivion.

At the end of the evening, there is a haunting passage in which one of the main characters, Mrs. Ramsay, realizes that, in a sense, the party is already gone: "With her foot on the threshold she waited a moment longer in a scene which was vanishing even as she looked, and then, as she moved and took Minta's arm and left the room, it changed, it shaped itself differently; it had become, she knew, giving one last look at it over her shoulder, already the past."[11]

Compare Woolf's dinner party with the account by the British poet W. H. Auden of an experience after a summer dinner that helped to bring him back to the Christian faith in which he had grown up:

> One fine summer night in June 1933 I was sitting on a lawn after dinner with three colleagues, two women and one man. We liked each other well enough, but we were certainly not intimate friends. . . . We were talking casually about everyday matters when quite suddenly and unexpectedly . . . I felt myself invaded by a power which, though I consented to it, was irresistible and certainly not mine. For the first time in my life I knew exactly . . . what it means to love one's neighbor as oneself. I was certain, though the conversation continued to be perfectly ordinary, that my three colleagues were having the same experience. . . . My personal feelings towards them were unchanged—they were still colleagues, not intimate friends—but I felt their existences of themselves to be of infinite value and rejoiced in it.

Auden goes on to reflect further on the meaning and extent of that experience:

> I recalled with shame the many occasions on which I had been spiteful, snobbish, selfish, but the immediate joy was greater than the shame, for I knew that, so long as I was possessed by this spirit, it would be literally impossible for me deliberately to injure another human being. I also knew that the power would, of course, be withdrawn sooner or later and that, when it did, my greed and self-regard would return. The experience . . . did not vanish completely for two days or so. The memory of the experience has not prevented me from making use of others, grossly and often,

but it has made it much more difficult for me to deceive myself about what I am up to when I do.[12]

For Auden, the encounter with this loving power was something dynamic, a hint at something transcendent and unwavering. Auden felt as though a very real power had acted upon him and brought him a kind of revelation or disclosure: the infinite value of his companions. It is interesting that while reflection on this experiential disclosure of love was part of the process that brought Auden to Christian faith, the experience took place at a time when he was quite skeptical about Christianity and religious faith in general. His encounter is very much in keeping with Cambridge Platonist spirituality.[13] The Cambridge Platonist Ralph Cudworth believed that more is needed to come to an awareness of God than scholarship or the intellect. There is an essential experiential element.

> Ink and paper can never make us Christians, can never make a new nature, a living principle in us, can never form Christ, or any true notions of spiritual things in our hearts. . . . Cold theorems and maxims, dry and jejune disputes, lean syllogistical reasonings could never yet of themselves beget the least glimpse of true heavenly light, the least sap of saving knowledge in any heart.[14]

Instead, Cudworth writes, "The secret mysteries of a divine life" must be "kindled from within" the soul.[15]

Golden Cords

The title of this book is derived from the several poems and stories in which a person in peril or on a quest must follow a cord or string in order to find the way to happiness or safety or home. One of the most famous of such tales involves the ancient Greek hero, Theseus, who sails to the island of Crete to kill the Minotaur, half bull, half human, who is to be found in a great labyrinth. Ariadne, the daughter of the king, falls in love with Theseus and gives him a ball of string as well as a knife. Theseus unrolls the ball to mark his way in to the labyrinth so that after he kills the Minotaur, he can find his way out. One of the great British poets, William Blake, used the metaphor of a golden string, which, if followed aright, will lead us to heaven itself. In "Jerusalem," Blake writes:

> I give you the end of a golden string,
>   Only wind it into a ball;
> It will lead you in at Heaven's gate,
>   Built in Jerusalem's wall.[16]

Auden's experience of love might plausibly be seen as such a golden string or cord.

I would love to begin this book by sketching and then defending a robust view of religious experience, a viewpoint that would fill out Auden's premonition that summer evening when he may have encountered divine love. But, if this book truly is to reply to the secular naturalist perspective, the starting point has to be further back. One cannot very well have a confident view that persons may experience the divine if one does not believe that persons and experiences exist! Thus, the first topic to be considered in chapter 1 is the existence of consciousness itself. Today there is heated debate over the reality and nature of conscious experience. I argue in chapters 1 through 3 that consciousness, personal identity, and experience give us some clues that theism (the thesis that there is an all-good, omnipotent, omniscient, omnipresent Creator whose existence is necessary or noncontingent) is viable in today's intellectual climate. The Cambridge Platonists rightly held (to my mind) that our concept of God and our concept of human nature are intertwined. They did not picture God as superhuman or some kind of projection of human attributes, but they held that God and creatures do have *some* powers in common, such as agency, love, and knowledge, and they also held that if one denies God's existence, then one has difficulty in recognizing human agency, and knowledge, and consciousness. For them, the recognition of consciousness—human and divine—stands or falls together. In the first chapters of this book, I suggest that the Cambridge Platonists are on the right track.

Also, in chapters 1 through 3 I am concerned about the existence and nature of the self. It may seem surprising to those not in professional philosophy, but some philosophers today argue that the self does not exist. Some philosophers may put the point forward in a way that seems merely technical, for instance, "human beings are not substantial selves who endure over time." But some, such as the British philosopher Susan Blackmore, are more straightforward. She disparages the idea of you and me as substantial selves as a delusion, and she denies both the self and our powers to act with freedom. She acknowledges the apparent existence of the self, but she believes that a properly neurologically-informed philosophy calls the self into question. Blackmore writes, "I long ago concluded that there is no substantial or persistent self to be found in experience, let alone in the brain. I have become quite uncertain as to whether there really is anything it is like to be me."[17] In a sense, writing and reading this book now has a modest, nonviolent analogy with conditions that George Orwell identified in his classic essay, "The Lion and the Unicorn," written during the Second World War. In perhaps the greatest first line in an essay, Orwell begins: "As I write, highly civilized human beings are flying overhead, trying to kill me."[18] I would adjust this slightly: As I write, highly gifted, scientifically informed philosophers are arguing that the concept of the self as a unified individual being existing over time is a delusion.

Golden Cords Leading to Eternity

The ultimate goal of this short book is to explore and vindicate the experience of God as an eternal, good being. Some philosophers may be disappointed, however, to find that a book on God's eternity will not seek to settle the question of whether God is outside of all time and thus outside the temporal passage from the past to the future. The book is neutral over the vexing philosophical arguments both pro and con. Most of the classical theologians in the Christian tradition (such as Boethius, Augustine, Anselm, and Aquinas) have held that God transcends time: God is eternal insofar as there is no before, during, or after, for God. In this view, time itself may be seen as a creation of God. Alternatively, some contemporary Christian theists interpret God's eternity in terms of God being everlasting. God's existence has no temporal origin or beginning and will have no end. And yet, God is not timeless or atemporal. Some advocates of this position speak of God as being in a "time beyond time," enjoying duration (a past, present, and future) but not as in the metric time of calendars or atomic clocks employed at the human level.[19] This book is compatible with either position. (Today, definitions of "eternity," derived from *aeturnus* in Latin, which is itself derived from *aevum*, "an era or time," are usually also neutral between an *eternal* God being timeless or in time but without beginning or end.) Both positions agree that, as Tatian the Syrian (second century) put it succinctly, "Our God has no introduction in time."[20] The experiences of God as *eternal* to be investigated in this book will refer to that mode of life and experience to which some of the great Christian mystics have testified, in which the encounter with God utterly subordinates temporal and transient matters to the superabundant, boundless life and love of God. Part of the project of this book will be to approach and explore such experiences. As an example of these sorts of experiences, consider this testimony of the contemporary Welsh poet R. S. Thomas:

> As with St. John the Divine on the island of Patmos I was 'in the Spirit' and I had a vision, in which I could comprehend the breadth and length and depth and height of the mystery of the creation. . . . I realized there was really no such thing as time, no beginning and no end but that everything is a fountain welling up endlessly from immortal God. There was certainly something in the place that gave me this feeling. The chapel stood in the fields, amidst the waving grass, its roof covered with a layer of yellow lichen. There were tall nettles growing around and at its side there swayed a big old tree like someone leaning forward to listen to the sermon. . . . It might have been the first day of Creation and myself one of the first men. . . . The dew of its [the world's] creation was on everything, and I fell to my knees and praised God—a young man worshipping a young God, for surely that is what our God is.[21]

Thomas does testify that in this experience "there was really no such thing as time," and yet such an experience does not seem frozen or unchanging but *dynamic*. He is awestruck by God's fecundity as a "fountain welling up endlessly," and he is enamored by "tall nettles growing"; neither *welling* nor *growing* makes sense unless there is movement and change. Thus, the experience of God's creativity is so awesome that it overwhelms our chronicles and clocks, our sense of one day following another (the kind of sentiment that partly laments the mere passage of time as in "the sun also rises," Eccles. 1:5).

Thomas's vision of God as young resonates with Augustine's recognition and praise of God as ever new. In the *Confessions*, Augustine refers to God: "Beauty at once so ancient and so new!"[22] Note that he does not refer to God as *ancient*. The implication rather is that God is ever new, both in ancient days as well as now. As it happens, Augustine believes firmly that God transcends time, and I will not challenge the classical view of divine atemporality. But I will be highlighting the dynamic, rapturous experience that Augustine and other mystics report, leaving it open whether God is atemporal or everlasting, without beginning or end.[23]

The contemporary philosophical literature on God's relationship to time is fascinating, but it is often abstract, drawing on concepts in physics and metaphysics with not a few technicalities. What seems missing is an appreciation that the early work on time by Christian thinkers was often very much linked to meditations on the glory of God and the comparative transience of worldly goods. The classical early text on God's relationship to time is Boethius' *On the Consolation of Philosophy*. Philosophers have concentrated on his claims about time and eternity, God's present, and so on, but Boethius' chief goal, which is underappreciated, was to critique worldly prestige, the pursuit of reputation, and living by and for transient glory. In this book I engage in philosophical reflection on human nature (as did Boethius), but my intent is to build up a conception of the eternal God whose love can truly transform our lives into what the Cambridge Platonists saw as fullness of life. This testimony of fullness and regenerative, transcendent love of God is quite the opposite of a remark attributed to Ludwig Wittgenstein, who wondered whether God might half exist.

The original context of the remark is lost, but for Augustine, the Cambridge Platonists, and R. S. Thomas, God's reality is the most real we can encounter; God is that fullness of being from which the cosmos derives its existence and continuation. In comparison with God, it is we who might half exist until we encounter God.[24]

Whether this vision of God is delusional or reliable is the central question in what follows. I shall be arguing in favor of its reliability, and I shall identify three important facets of the experience of and reflection about God as eternal: it calls for the subordination of what may be called temporal or material glory (the pursuit of earthly power and fame); it involves realizing that God is the God of irrepressible life; and it involves a recognition of the hallowed nature of domestic virtue. These claims will be unpacked and explored in the last two chapters.

While this book builds a case for golden cords leading to fullness of being, there will also be attention to quite the opposite. Sometimes minor acts or incidental gestures can lead one to great perils and alienation from the fullness of life. A brief example will have to suffice. Consider Stendhal's novel *The Red and the Black*. One of its central characters, Julien Sorel, seeks to seduce Madame de Rénal. At first, he is intent on holding her hand in the presence of her husband:

> The darkness hid every movement. He ventured to place his hand close to the pretty arm which her gown left bare. Troubled, no longer conscious of what he was doing, he moved his cheek in the direction of this pretty arm, and made bold to press his lips to it.
>
> Madame de Rénal shuddered. Her husband was a few feet away, she hastened to give Julian her hand, at the same time, thrusting him slightly from her. While Monsieur de Rénal continued his abuse of the good-for-nothings and Jacobins who were making fortunes, Julian covered the hand which had been left in his with passionate kisses, or so at least they seemed by Madame de Rénal.[25]

Perhaps a trivial act, but it ultimately leads to murder and utter disaster—indeed, the opposite of a golden cord and more like the first step in tying a hangman's knot.

Situating the Current Project

In some respects this book is a prequel. In 2005, I published a collection of essays, written in the creative nonfiction genre, called *Love, Love, Love and Other Essays: Light Reflections on Love, Life, and Death.*[26] The title was taken from the essay "Love, Love, Love." This was a short meditation on my father's death: his last words to me repeated "love" three times (my father, ninety-five years old, was inspired by the advice in the fourteenth-century mystical text, *The Cloud of Unknowing*, which recommends repeated use of the word "Love"). In this book, however, the chapters are set forth sequentially to systematically explore the Cambridge Platonist philosophy of life over against secular naturalism. Also the *Love, Love, Love* book is, as one of my students put it, more ecstatic than backed up by arguments. She suggested that it was written (in the words of Athenagoras of Athens, second century) "in an ecstasy beyond the natural powers of reasoning." *The Golden Cord* is different: while I have tried to include some elements of "creative nonfiction," and there may be an ecstatic utterance or two, there are more arguments to consider.

The Golden Cord is written for Christian as well as non-Christian readers. No more philosophy is presupposed than what you will find in Daniel Dennett's *Breaking the Spell*. While *The Golden Cord* might well be entitled *Weaving the Spell* (Dennett seeks to break the spell or apparent attraction of theism, whereas my aim is to highlight the lure and enchantment of theism), it is more of an inquiry that I invite you to undertake, rather than apologetics or a textbook of arguments.[27] (I have developed arguments for theism systematically elsewhere.)[28] In this book I do defend the coherence of theism and offer some reasons for resisting materialism and for trusting religious experience. But these are all undertaken to fill out the thesis that life may contain golden cords that lead you to the God of Eternal love, rather than as part of an academic enterprise. For non-Christian readers, my hope is that you will be inclined to say about this thesis (to borrow a line from a philosopher friend), "Well, maybe." I do not think the arguments presented in what follows are of decisive, unanswerable force, but I believe they have merit in providing good reasons for embracing a Cambridge Platonist spirituality. And for readers who are already Christian, my hope is that you will find proposals and positions that call for further (and better) exploration.

An important further preparatory note is in order. Some Christian thinkers today see Christianity and Platonism as bad bedfellows. Platonism is associated with a body-denigrating dualism of soul and body (soul = good; body = bad) in which nature and this life are a mere shadowland of true life, unencumbered by the material world. Platonism has also been associated with an unhealthy valorization of reason over against desire. The Christian Platonism championed by the heroes of *The Golden Cord* is not guilty: while the Cambridge Platonists thought that materialism is false (the soul is not the very same thing as one's body), they argued for the good of *embodied* life, the goodness of creation (the material and immaterial world), the central value of a passionate love for the good, the true, and the beautiful. And insofar as they believed in the afterlife, they saw it as a miracle rather than something that occurs willy-nilly due to the innate power of the soul.

Because this book is not a text in the technical Platonic scholarship, readers will need to look elsewhere for a closer look at the historical Plato and the many movements and ideas that he inspired. For now, I ask readers to set aside some of the commonplace and ill-earned associations with Platonism as chapter 1 begins with considerations of love and life in the current intellectual climate as well as in the physical world. The first chapter addresses the most substantial obstacle to the project of *The Golden Cord*. In that chapter as well as in some of the others, I liberally cite the writings of other philosophers so that readers can engage with their thinking on their own terms, not always by way of a paraphrase.

CHAPTER 1

LOVE IN THE PHYSICAL WORLD

Midway this way of life we're bound upon,
I woke to find myself in a dark wood,
Where the right road was wholly lost and gone.
—Dante, *Inferno*

When I was in my twenties, a graduate student at Harvard University and not yet midway on life's journey, I attended a philosophy seminar on the nature of language, with a focus on metaphor. The professor requested that we come up with a sentence that expressed obvious nonsense. The usual example employed in many texts at the time was Noam Chomsky's great line, "Colorless green ideas sleep furiously." Rather than invoke green ideas, the professor wrote on the blackboard: "Gravity is a manifestation of love." There was some forced laughter, though I felt a little uneasy when I realized that I actually believed that this "obvious nonsense" was true and foundational to life itself.

At the time, I was in a Dante reading group (about twelve of us met on Sunday nights in a tiny apartment on Beacon Hill in Boston to read out loud and discuss Dante's *Divine Comedy* over wine). Perhaps my professor came up with his example of "obvious nonsense" after seeing my T-shirt, which featured a reprint of Gustave Doré's illustration of the Beatific Vision (the "Celestial Rose") and the famous last lines of the *Paradiso*: "My will and my desire were turned by love, / The love that moves the sun and the other stars."[1]

Before reveling in Dante's vision of love and delving into the ways in which earthly love may provide a path into eternal, divine love, we need to explore why such a divine expedition seems to many philosophers absolutely preposterous and pathetic. Without a plausible challenge to the rather hostile state of play in some quarters of the world of philosophy, the task of this book will seem like a fool's errand.

Intellectual Climates

Graduate schools, and universities in general, have their own atmosphere. At Harvard, at least in the philosophy department or, more specifically, in the seminars and classes I took in the 1970s, the atmosphere was decidedly materialistic. "Materialism" can be described variously as the view either that *all that exists is in space and time* or that *all that exists can ultimately be explained by the physical sciences*, and so on. Exact definitions are not crucial here, except to highlight the form of materialism that lay behind my professor's choice of examples. At Harvard in the 1960s and 1970s, the great Willard van Orman Quine argued that, ultimately, references to mental realities such as beliefs, desires, and so on (including references to love) should give way to a vocabulary of science that lacked such terms. As a friend of B. F. Skinner, Quine preferred behaviorist accounts of human action. Daniel Dennett captures the mood of the time:

> The prevailing wisdom, variously expressed and argued for, is *materialism*: there is only one sort of stuff, namely *matter*—the physical stuff of

physics, chemistry, and physiology—and the mind is somehow nothing but a physical phenomenon. In short, the mind is the brain. According to the materialists, we can (in principle!) account for every mental phenomenon using the same physical principles, laws and raw materials that suffice to explain radioactivity, continental drift, photosynthesis, reproduction, nutrition, and growth.[2]

While I postpone at the outset any serious questioning of this "wisdom," note that Dennett defines the material in terms of physical sciences—physics, chemistry, physiology. Perhaps under "physiology," the scientific study of the function of living systems, Dennett would include a wide array of disciplines, but noticeably absent from Dennett's explicit identification of alpha modes of cognition are, for example, psychology, sociology, and history. It is perhaps not surprising that philosophy and theology are excluded, but Dennett seems to be more confident in the reality of explanatory significance of the "physical principles, laws and raw materials that suffice to explain radioactivity, continental drift, photosynthesis, reproduction, nutrition, and growth" than in the reality and explanatory power of "mental phenomenon." But doesn't the very process of science and the practice of explaining things and forming concepts of laws involve or even presuppose "mental phenomenon"? Presumably, physicists, chemists, and physiologists have to have conscious experiences, beliefs, and desires to practice their disciplines. I leave this suggestion here as merely an observation that Dennett (and some other materialists) employ a methodology that does not begin with the mental, but that does begin with a confident, perhaps "objective" view of physical laws and principles. Later, I will question the wisdom of this starting point.

Materialism is often advanced as itself a thoroughly scientific claim. D. M. Armstrong even describes materialism as a scientific "doctrine":

> What does modern science have to say about the nature of man? There are, of course, all sorts of disagreements and divergencies in the views of individual scientists. But I think it is true to say that one view is steadily gaining ground, so that it bids fair to become established scientific doctrine. This is the view that we can give a complete account of man *in*

purely physico-chemical terms. . . . I think it is fair to say that those scientists who still reject the physico-chemical account of man do so primarily for philosophical, or moral or religious reasons, and only secondarily, and half-heartedly, for reasons of scientific detail. . . .

For me, then, and for many philosophers who think like me, the moral is clear. We must try to work out an account of the nature of mind which is compatible with the view that man is nothing but a physico-chemical mechanism.[3]

Like Dennet, Armstrong is clear about his starting point and orientation. Among the remarkable things in Armstrong's charge is that he is presenting materialism not as a philosophy of science but as itself a scientific thesis. If Armstrong is right, then science (to use his metaphor) *says* that materialism is true.

Some materialists are at home with allowing that there are such things as conscious states, feelings, desires, and so on, but they claim that these turn out to be material states. Yet other materialists, such as Dennett (though hard to pin down), Quine, Stephen Stich, Paul Churchland, and Patricia Churchland wind up eliminating the mental as we usually think of it in terms of their final account of what exists.

The British philosopher Alistair Hannay has a great image of the attitude of contemporary materialists (also called physicalists):

The attitude of much physicalism [to consciousness] has been that of new owners to a sitting tenant. They would prefer eviction but, failing that, are content to dispose of as much of the paraphernalia as possible while keeping busy in other parts of the house. We should, I think, feel free to surmise that the current picture of consciousness eking out a sequestered life as a print-out monitor or raw feeler fails in a quite radical way to capture the facts.[4]

Using this schema, my professor and his colleagues preferred evicting consciousness and the mental, while other materialists only allow for marginal mental entities. In this chapter let us consider the more radical materialists.

The Radical Materialist Temptation

Stich and many of the other radical materialists refer to our usual or ordinary concepts of the mental as *folk psychology*. They think that just as the sciences have come to see that folk astronomy is false, the same could be true for folk psychology—our commonplace assumption that there are beliefs, desires, and so on. According to Stich,

> Folk astronomy was false astronomy and not just in detail. The general conception of the cosmos embedded in the folk wisdom of the West was utterly and thoroughly mistaken. Much the same could be said for folk biology, folk chemistry, and folk physics. However wonderful and imaginative folk theorizing and speculation has been, it has turned out to be screamingly false in every domain where we now have a reasonably sophisticated science. Nor is there any reason to think that ancient camel drivers would have greater insight or better luck when the subject at hand was the structure of their own minds rather than the structure of matter or of the cosmos.[5]

Paul Churchland takes a similar stance. He thinks that our recognition of beliefs, desires, and the like might be on a par with the older practice of thinking that there are witches:

> Witches provide another example. Psychosis is a fairly common affliction among humans, and in earlier centuries its victims were standardly seen as cases of demonic possession, as instances of Satan's spirit itself, glaring malevolently out at us from behind the victims' eyes. That witches exist was not a matter of any controversy. One would occasionally see them, in any city or hamlet, engaged in incoherent, paranoid, or even murderous behavior. But observable or not, we eventually decided that witches simply do not exist. We concluded that the concept of a witch is an element in a conceptual framework that misrepresents so badly the phenomena to which it was standardly applied that literal application of the notion should be permanently withdrawn. Modern theories of mental dysfunction led to the elimination of witches from our serious ontology.

The concepts of folk psychology—belief, desire, fear, sensation, pain, joy, and so on—await a similar fate.[6]

Note the radical nature of this daring possibility. Could it be that we need to abandon a framework that recognizes beliefs, desires, fears, pains, and joys? If we abandon such notions, it will not make sense to claim that we *believe* in this new framework that treats beliefs like witches. To claim that we believe there are no beliefs would be like claiming that lots of witches think that good witches should claim that there are no witches. If we are going to get rid of both witches and beliefs, we need to let both go.

A classic example of the elimination of the mental was embraced by Richard Rorty in the 1960s. He thought that we might one day give up on our folk psychology:

> The absurdity of saying "Nobody has ever felt a pain" is not greater than that of saying "Nobody has ever seen a demon," if we have a suitable answer to the question, "What was I reporting when I said I felt a pain?" To this question, the science of the future may reply, "You were reporting the occurrence of a certain brain process, and it would make life simpler for us if you would, in the future say "My C-fibres are firing," instead of saying "I'm in pain."[7]

In this view, we may replace mental language with references to brain and other bodily processes. This radical elimination of the mental (or at least its radical retranslation into neurological terms) has been called *eliminativism*. Its high view of science has been labeled *scientism*. Jerry Fodor is prepared to use this term in describing his stance:

> I hold to the philosophical view that, for want of a better term, I'll call by one that is usually taken to be pejorative: *Scientism*. Scientism claims, on the one hand, that the goals of scientific inquiry include the discovery of objective empirical truths; and on the other hand, that science has come pretty close to achieving this goal at least from time to time. The molecular theory of gasses, I suppose, is a plausible example of achieving it in physics; so is cell theory in biology; the theory, in geology, that the earth is

very old; and the theory, in astronomy, that the stars are very far away. . . . I'm inclined to think that Scientism, so construed, is not just true but *obviously and certainly* true; it's something that nobody in the late twentieth century who has a claim to an adequate education and a minimum of common sense should doubt.[8]

To fully get to *radical* materialism, however, one needs a minor addition: the sciences are our only means of knowing about ourselves and the world. So confident is Peter Ungar that a bond exists between faith in science and adherence to physicalism that he has coined the term *scientificalism.*[9]

One of the most popular of the radical materialists is Daniel Dennett, as mentioned above. In the following passage he blasts ("reproaches" seems too tame a word) David Chalmers for proposing that *experience* should be taken to be a fundamental datum, a fact to be explained. For Dennett, experience may turn out to be an element of folk psychology that we should banish from our final account of what exists. He thinks Chalmers's confidence that experience is a datum is equivalent to claiming that the property "cuteness" must exist:

> We can see this by comparing Chalmers' proposal with yet one more imaginary non-starter; *cutism*, the proposal that since some things are just plain cute, and other things aren't cute at all—you can just see it, however hard it is to describe or explain—we had better postulate *cuteness* as a fundamental property of physics alongside mass, charge, and space-time. (Cuteness is *not* a functional property, of course; I can imagine somebody who wasn't actually cute at all but who nevertheless functioned exactly as if cute—trust me.) Cutism is in even worse shape than vitalism. [A discredited scientific theory that life functions in virtue of a vital principle of energy not reducible to the laws of chemistry and physics.] Nobody would have taken vitalism seriously for a minute if the vitalists hadn't had a set of independently describable phenomena—of reproduction, metabolism, self-repair and the like—that their postulated fundamental life-element was hoped to account for. Once these phenomena were otherwise accounted for, vitalism fell flat, but at least it had a project. Until Chalmers gives an independent ground for contemplating the drastic

move of adding "experience" to mass, charge, and space-time, his proposal is one that can be put on the back burner.[10]

Dennett maintains that we can be more certain that mass, charge, and space-time exists than we can be sure that experience exists.

Unlike Dennett, some materialists seem to not see a problem in affirming a strong form of materialism and affirming the reality of experience. One popular writer and materialist who takes this position is Carl Sagan:

> I am a collection of water, calcium, and organic molecules called Carl Sagan. You are a collection of almost identical molecules with a different collective label. But is that all? Is there nothing in here but molecules? Some people find this idea somehow demeaning to human dignity. For myself, I find it elevating that our universe permits the evolution of molecular machines as intricate and subtle as we. But the essence of life is not so much the atoms and simple molecules that make us up as the way in which they are put together.[11]

The question then is: can the following identity be secured? *Feeling elated is the very same thing as molecular activity.*

Identity Problems

The reason why the more radical materialists worry about elevated feelings—joy and sorrow and beliefs—is because if you acknowledge them as full-fledged experiential states (sometimes called phenomenal states), it becomes difficult to see how they could be the very same things as a pack of neurons or molecular processes or the body and its processes as a whole. It seems as though you could know all about the molecular structure and physical processes of bodily life and know nothing of the experiential states involved, and vice versa. The difficulty at hand becomes apparent when you consider other identity relationships, cases in which you have only one object but two ways of identifying it. Take "water" and "H_2O." These two terms pick out the same thing, and once we grasp atomic theory we may see that water is H_2O; to know about water is to know about H_2O. Philosophers have formulated what they call the principle of the indiscernability of identicals:

If A is B, whatever is true of A is true of B

Consider these identity relations:

The morning Star is the Evening Star
Water is H_2O
Cassius Clay is Muhammad Ali
Bayer Aspirin is acetylsalicylic acid
Mark Twain is Samuel Clemens

In the case of each, whatever is true of one (the Morning Star is Venus) is true of the other (the Evening Star is Venus). And whatever is true of Muhammad Ali (known by you to be a famous boxer) is true of Cassius Clay (known by you to be a famous boxer even if you don't know him by the name of Cassius Clay).[12] If you are boxing with Muhammad Ali, you are boxing with Cassius Clay, and so on. Now, consider the following. Feeling elated is the very same thing as the physical-chemical processes in the brain. Bear in mind that this claim involves strict identity (as with the other examples) and not merely attribution, as when I claim that the dog Tiepolo is black and white. We cannot thereby claim that if you have a black and white creature, then you have Tiepolo (you may instead have the dog Jack). In cases of strict identity, however, there is a one-to-one identity, as in *water is the very same thing as H_2O*. In the case of identifying feelings and physical chemical processes in the brain, we have a problem, for as Colin McGinn puts it, "the property of consciousness itself (or specific conscious states) is not an observable or perceptible property of the brain. You can stare into a living conscious brain, your own or someone else's, and see there a wide variety of instantiated properties—its shape, colour, texture, etc.—but you will not thereby see what the subject is experiencing, the conscious state itself."[13]

Is whatever that is true of *feeling elated* also true of the physical-chemical processes to which it is supposed to be identical? It at least appears not, for (to restate the earlier point) you could (in principle) know all about the physical-chemical processes of a person's body and not know anything at all about the person's emotional or mental state, and vice versa. In regard to the other identity cases, we do not have this problem. One can fully grasp that water is H_2O—this is a simple statement of composition—but we do not have this with the mental and physical. Richard Swinburne puts the problem facing materialism in this way: "I argue . . . that knowledge of what happens to bodies and their parts, and knowledge of the mental events which occur in connection with them will not suffice to give you knowledge of what happens to those persons who are (currently) men. Talk about persons is not analysable in terms of talk about bodies and their connected mental life."[14]

I suggest that Swinburne has a good point. Some philosophers claim that the identity of the mental and physical is no more puzzling than the identity of digestion with the different enzymes and organs involved or between heat and mean kinetic energy. But in the first case, once you know all about the enzymes and organs, you know all there is about digestion, and yet this is not the case of the mental. You might have an exhaustive physical analysis of the brain and body of a person and yet not know his mental states. Consciousness and different mental states can be inferred, projected, and grasped based on a person's testimony and on studying correlations of bodily states and mental states of other subjects and their testimony, but this is not a matter of seeing that the bodily states are identical to mental states. Materialists such as Frank Jackson have objected that our understanding of the brain could become so advanced that we can *deduce* a person's mental state (what he is thinking/feeling) from his brain state. Daniel von Wachter responds:

> Regardless of how plausible it is that the psychological is deducible from the physical in the way Jackson describes, he fails to address the crucial point. Of course, if materialism is true and if you know what kind of brain state underlies every kind of mental state, then from this information (which you may call "contextual information"), given a description

of my brain in physical terms, you can deduce what my mental life is like. Nevertheless, the point is that you cannot deduce it from the description of my brain *without* this contextual information. No description of my body in physical terms tells you whether I have a red image in my mind, or whether I have a headache, or whether I am thinking hard about whether 371 is a prime number.[15]

Swinburne argues that so-called scientific materialists who recognize the existence of sensations confuse causal interaction with identity. The fact that the mental and physical impact each other (say, a blow to the head causes one to lose consciousness) is no reason to think that the mental *is* physical:

> My sensations are no doubt *caused by* brain-events but they are not *themselves* brain-events. My having a red after-image or a pain or a smell of roast beef are real events. If science describes only firings of neurons in the brain, it has not told us everything that is going on. For it is a further fact about the world that there are pains and after-images, and science must state this fact and attempt to explain it. Likewise sensations are to be distinguished from the behaviour to which they give no expression—pains which they conceal or dream-sensations which they report to no one— and, if the sensations give rise to behaviour, the subject is aware of the sensation as a separate event from the behaviour to which it gives rise. The life of conscious experience seems a reality ignored by hard materialism.[16]

The full acknowledgment of the reality of consciousness causes some materialists to wonder whether we will ever come to understand how it is that mental states (say, like feeling elated) could be the same as physical states. Michael Lockwood writes:

> I count myself a materialist, in the sense that I take consciousness to be a species of brain activity. Having said that, however, it seems to me evident that no description of brain activity of the relevant kind, couched in the currently available languages of physics, physiology, or functional or computational roles, is remotely capable of capturing what is distinctive about

consciousness. So glaring, indeed, are the shortcomings of all the reductive programmes currently on offer, that I cannot believe that anyone with a philosophical training, looking dispassionately at these programmes, would take any of them seriously for a moment, were it not for a deep-seated conviction that current physical science has essentially got reality taped, and accordingly, *something* along the lines of what the reductionists are offering must be correct. To that extent the very existence of consciousness seems to me to be a standing demonstration of the explanatory limitations of contemporary physical science.[17]

Consider an objection: But couldn't the apparent difficulty arise simply because our mental terms (joy, sorrow) are just part of how we know about physical-chemical states? One thing can be known in more than one way. For example, I might know you as my sister's best friend, but I do not know that you are a secret agent. The pack of neurons or physical processes unique to Sagan might be known by way of certain mental concepts, and yet this is not evidence that Sagan is more than a pack of neurons.

The difficulty here, though, lies in the fact that when it comes to the mental, *how it appears* is a central feature of its nature. Feeling elated, like feeling pain, joy, and so on, is a *way of experiencing*. So there is a disanalogy with the case of the sister analogy—we may easily see how a single person may appear differently, and we can even see that these two appearances are different (*being a sister's best friend* is not the same as *being a spy*). When it comes to the physical-chemical processes, however, there is nothing about these processes that we can observe as appearing elated or any such mental state. Dennett's effort to claim that it only appears that there are appearances seems to collapse because it implicitly requires there to be appearances in the first place. T. L. S. Sprigge aptly observes that we can be certain of the reality of our conscious thinking, even if we are mistaken about what we are thinking:

Let us consider first the implications of saying that it *is* logically possible that one's consciousness, over a lifetime, might thus be totally delusive. It remains true, nonetheless, that the fact that the precise series of experiences has taken place is a fact which includes, or logically implies, a whole lot of things as to what you have thought to be the case. It might include, for example, the fact that you were once thinking it the case that your daughter was on a train to York. That is, it does not really make sense to think that, after a long stretch of experience, it is an open question what, on various occasions, you were thinking.[18]

As a character in Charles Williams's novel *The Shadows of Ecstasy* reflects, on the evident character of appearances:

> A thing that seemed had at least the truth of its seeming. Sir Bernard's mind refused to allow it more but it also refused to allow it less. It was for each man to determine how urgent the truth of each seeming was. . . . A thing might not be true because it appeared so to him, but it was no less likely to be true because everyone else denied it. The eyes of Rosamond might or might not hold the secret origin of day and night, but if they apparently did then they apparently did, and it would be silly to deny it and equally silly not to relish it.[19]

Some materialists who recognize the difficulty of identifying feelings and other mental states with brain activity resort to the concept of representations. They agree that our feeling elated seems unique and perhaps immaterial, but it is actually a mental representation of a fundamentally physical reality. Feeling pain, then, may constitute how we represent some physical process. These materialists concede that mental terms are words that mean something different from physical terms, but they both refer to the same physical phenomenon. And yet the difficulty remains: so long as one does not eliminate *how pain or being elated feels*, those feelings must be recognized as *real states and activities*. One does not feel the concept of pain; rather, one undergoes the feeling itself. Thus, when you or I report that we are feeling pain, the feeling itself is the content and meaning of our report. If someone replies, "It would be better if you simply reported that brain activity X is taking place," this different form of reporting would do nothing to alleviate what is crucial: *how you feel*, or, putting the point in a neurological context, *how your brain and central nervous system were making you feel.* Actually, the case for distinguishing the mental and physical can even be intensified beyond this knowledge argument (if the mental is the physical, to know one is to know the other). One may also entertain the following: *it is possible to have all the physical-chemical processes specified by Sagan but have no mental life at all.* Admittedly, this would be a bizarre case of what may be called a zombie, a creature that acts and looks like it is thinking and feeling but is not. The idea of a zombie is more at home in science fiction than in a laboratory, but the apparent coherence of such a creature is a challenge to those who embrace an identity materialist theory.[20]

Let us consider such bizarre cases in the next chapter, but for now I simply note that it is a *possible* worry and a reason why some materialists are drawn to eliminate the mental altogether. Eliminating the mental is, however, not something one wants to do without seriously counting the cost. For many (but not all) philosophers, such an elimination would be like checking into a hospital in order to eliminate a headache through decapitation.

Going Shopping and the Deep Background

The reason why many people are drawn to getting rid of the mental is that if you recognize its existence, then you need to account for where it came from. A student of mine once put the point this way: "If the mental is different from the physical, how did the mental come into being? Did it go shopping?" Dennett and others posit a fundamentally physical world that is not, at its core, purposive or mental. For them, a genuine explanation of the world must ultimately describe it in terms that are nonintentional. There is no place to go outside the physical world to purchase nonphysical, intentional properties or things (souls). According to Dennett, "The account of intelligence required of psychology must not of course be question-begging. It must not explain intelligence in terms of intelligence, for instance by assigning responsibility for the existence of intelligence in creatures to the munificence of an intelligent Creator."[21] Moreover, George Rey has the same view: "Any ultimate explanation of mental phenomena will have to be in *non*-mental terms, or else it won't be an *explanation* of it. There might be explanations of some mental phenomena in terms of others—perhaps *hope* in terms of *belief* and *desire*—but if we are to provide an explanation of all mental phenomena, we would in turn have to explain such mentalistic explainers until finally we reached entirely non-mental terms."[22]

Later in chapter 3, we will explore the ways in which the Dennett-Rey strategy can be challenged by an alternative, broader framework. But for now I simply note that the motivation behind radical materialism is a strong drive to come up with a comprehensive philosophy that does not leave intelligence, consciousness, belief, and so on as irreducible realities. These phenomena all need to be explained in terms of nonintelligent, nonconscious forces. According to radical materialists, so long as we do not get underneath and account for how and where the self and the mental in general come from and are constituted, we have failed to explain the self. Dennett writes:

> In other words, the substantial self cannot form part of the final theory of what exists. "You've got to leave the first person [substantial self] out of your final theory. You won't have theory of consciousness if you still have the first person in there, because that was what it was your job to explain. All the paraphernalia that doesn't make any sense unless you've got a first person in there, has to be turned into something else. You've got to figure out some way to break it up and distribute its powers and opportunities in to the system in some other way."[23]

Dennett thereby seeks to get underneath the self or mind or subject as an independent, irreducible reality. Thus, he prefers to see the brain as a system without a subject:

> And the trouble with brains, it seems, is that when you look in them, you discover that *there's nobody home.* No part of the brain is the thinker that does the thinking or the feeler that does the feeling, and the whole brain appears to be no better a candidate for that very special role. This is a slippery topic. Do brains think? Do eyes see? Or do people see with their eyes

and think with their brains? Is there a difference? Is this just a trivial point of "grammar" or does it reveal a major source of confusion? The idea that a *self* (or a person, or, for that matter, a soul) is distinct from a brain or a body is deeply rooted in our ways of speaking, and hence in our ways of thinking.[24]

Perhaps the most sustained advocates of *eliminativism* are Paul Churchland and Patricia Churchland. In a book by Paul Churchland, *The Engine of Reason*, he warns that many of us who approach his book assume that there are such things as beliefs, desires, and the like:

> You came to this book assuming that the basic units of human cognition are states such as thoughts, beliefs, perceptions, desire, and preferences. That assumption is natural enough: it is built into the vocabulary of every natural language. . . . These assumptions are central elements in our standard conception of human cognitive activity, a conception often called 'folk psychology' to acknowledge it as the common property of folks generally. Their universality notwithstanding, these bedrock assumptions are probably mistaken.[25]

But, he continues, "Is our basic conception of human cognition and agency yet another myth, moderately useful in the past perhaps, yet false at edge or core? Will a proper theory of brain function present a significantly different or incompatible portrait of human nature? I am inclined toward positive answers to all of these questions."[26]

In such a world of elimination, it appears that not only might it be absurd to think that gravity is a manifestation of love, but love itself might be something that needs to be scrutinized as a dispensable, respectable category. In a famous paper, Rorty advocated such an elimination that is substantial: "Every speech, thought, theory, poem, composition and philosophy will turn out to be completely predictable in purely naturalistic terms. Some atoms-and-the-void account of micro-processes within individual human beings will permit the prediction of every sound or inscription which will ever be uttered. There are no ghosts."[27] On this view, rather than reporting to someone "I love you," perhaps one should say,

"My C-fibres are firing." Even uttering "My C-fibres are firing" will have been brought about by nonmental, unthinking causes.

What Happens to the Self on Dennett's View?

Dennett maintains that we must choose either materialism or dualism, the view that persons are nonphysical and yet embodied, but on his view dualism is utterly and completely a nonstarter: "This fundamentally anti-scientific stance of dualism is, to my mind, its most disqualifying feature, and is the reason why in this book I adopt the apparently dogmatic rule that dualism is to be avoided *at all costs*. It is not that I think I can give a knock-down proof that dualism, in all its forms, is false or incoherent, but that, given the way dualism wallows in mystery, *accepting dualism is giving up*."[28] Dualism is also unacceptable on scientific grounds:

> No physical energy or mass is associated with them [souls]. How, then, do they get to make a difference to what happens in the brain cells they must affect, if the mind is to have any influence over the body? A fundamental principle of physics is that any change in the trajectory of any physical entity is an acceleration requiring the expenditure of energy, and where is this energy to come from? It is this impossibility of "perpetual motion machines," and the same principle is apparently violated by dualism. This confrontation between quite standard physics and dualism has been end-lessly discussed since Descartes's own day, and is widely regarded as the inescapable and fatal flaw of dualism.[29]

According to Paul Churchland, dualism is incompatible with contemporary science: "It will be evident from the rest of this book that this familiar hypothesis [dualism] is difficult to square with the emerging theory of cognitive processes and with the experimental results from several neurosciences. The doctrine of an immaterial soul looks, to put it frankly, like just another myth, false not just at the edges, but to the core."[30] But if dualism does not provide grounds for selfhood, materialists such as Churchland are prepared to question the very existence of the self: "But who can be watching this pixilated show? The answer is straight-forward: no one. There is no distinct 'self' in there, beyond the brain as a whole. On the other hand, almost every part of the brain is being 'watched' by some other part of the brain, often by several other parts at once."[31]

Churchland does not see that eliminativism will threaten to bring in a loveless, mechanical worldview and, perhaps, to put on display his settled view on the compatibility of eliminativism and his philosophy of personal relations. He includes several personal allusions in *The Engine of Reason*. There is, for example, a photograph of his daughter and her "soulmate," which is then analyzed in terms of retina-visual cortex interaction. And there is an MRI image of Patricia Churchland's brain. Churchland comments: "This particular brain is in fact well known to me via more conventional information pathways. It is the brain of my wife and colleague, Patricia Churchland, and it is very dear to me." He even uses positive language of the soul in stating his final position: "One's first impulse, perhaps, is to see the vocabulary and framework of a general theory of the brain as something alien and cold. But it will not be alien if it depicts all of us, at last, as we truly are. . . . Whatever the distractions, we must continue to exercise our reason. And whatever the temptations we must continue to nurture our souls. That is why understanding the brain is so supremely important. It is the engine of reason. It is the seat of the soul."[32] Can Churchland retain all the emotion and passion of love if we do think that beliefs, desires, and so on, are part of a false framework?

Where Is the Love?

Let's assess the radical materialist stance. Can Paul Churchland have his eliminativism and the love of his life at the same time? Regrettably, it is not very clear how he can succeed both in advancing eliminativism and redeeming the promise that it will assist us in an effort to "nurture our souls" and care for one another. Obviously the brain sciences can assist us insofar as they enable us to treat physiological illnesses and the organic bases for psychological dysfunction. They provide the nonelimi-native philosopher with insights into the material underpinnings of our mental life. But it is not clear how we can make use of notions such as "assist," "care," and so forth, if we must shed bedrock assumptions about thoughts, beliefs, perceptions, desires, and preferences. In most if not all cases, "care," "compassion," and "love" make sense only within a conceptual context of beliefs and desires and preferences. At a minimum, love between persons seems to involve beliefs about oneself, beliefs about the beloved, and some concern for another's well-being. In *The Engine of Reason*, we are not given a clear guide as to how, in folk language, what we refer to as "love," "care," "compassion," and so on can be given any purchase in an eliminative world. These personal terms seem to be at the heart of the folk psychology that eliminativists are prepared to jettison, along with any talk of witches.

One of the problems facing the radical materialists is that they assume we have a clear, problem-free understanding of the physical world and face the puzzlement of trying to figure out how love and other mental states might fit in. Dennett and the Churchlands set up a supposedly problem-free picture of ourselves in the brain sciences and other physical sciences and then lampoon anyone who would seek to go beyond the physical sciences in an account of human life. Public Enemy Number One (for Dennett) is any form of dualism in which a person is seen as an embodied soul or mind or as a mixture of distinct properties, some physical, and some nonphysical. Following his teacher, Gilbert Ryle, Dennett depicts dualism as positing a kind of ghost in our bodies (to be explored in the next chapter).

But is the above intellectual climate the only one around? Or is it even stable? Consider Dennett's claim again that we should be skeptical about the existence of experience. But what is more evident: the fact that we have experiences, or the latest finding in theoretical physics? The latest physics seems anything but stable. Modern physics has certainly destabilized a commonsense concept of the material world, for, as Bertrand Russell once observed, "Matter has become as ghostly as anything in a spiritual séance."[33] More recently, and with a little less hyperbole, Noam Chomsky observed: "The supposed concepts of 'physical' or 'material' have no clear sense."[34] The prestigious *Oxford Companion to Philosophy* entry "Materialism" underscores the fluctuations in our concepts of the physical world and how these make materialism as a theory less clear and commonsensical:

> Materialism. Basically the view that everything is made of matter. But what is matter? Probably the most innocent and cheerful acceptance of it comes right at the start of materialism with Democritus of Abdera (in northern Greece) in the fifth century BC, for whom the world consisted entirely of 'atoms', tiny, absolutely hard, impenetrable, incompressible, indivisible and unalterable bits of 'stuff', which had shape and size but no other properties and scurried around in the void, forming the world as we know it by jostling each other and either rebounding (despite being incompressible) or getting entangled with each other because of their shapes. They and the void alone were real, the colours and flavours and temperatures that surround us being merely subjective...This model has lasted, with various modifications and sophistications, right down until modern times, though the notion of solidity was causing qualms at least as early as Locke. But in the last century all has been thrown into confusion by Einstein's famous $E = mc2$ and also by general relativity. . . .
>
> All this, however, has had remarkably little overt effect on the various philosophical views that can be dubbed 'materialism', though *one might think it shows at least that materialism is not the simple no-nonsense, tough-minded alternative it might once have seemed to be* [emphasis mine].[35]

In light of such changes, it is difficult to plausibly claim, as Dennett does, that we should be more confident in the posits of contemporary physics than confident that conscious experience exists. In fact, it is hard (nearly impossible, I suggest) to imagine any science at all unless one recognizes the existence of experience. After all, isn't scientific inquiry based on multiple, repeatable *conscious experiences* that scientists codify and research? Rather than begin with the physical sciences, why not begin with the fact that there are scientists? I assume that scientists exist and that they have experiences and engage in inquiry; they have beliefs about the brain, human anatomy in general, and so on. Let's further assume that authors such as Dennett exist and write books for good reasons. I suggest that in philosophy one's starting point is vital, and if we are looking for the least problematic starting point, why not assume that there is thinking, experiencing, and assuming?

Thus, rather than begin with the brain sciences and then ask about ghosts, why not begin with the self and ask how the brain sciences can illuminate or help account for our life of thinking, feeling, having emotions and values? I suggest that we begin with what Quine and others call the mental (the fact that we experience, have feelings, and so on). This preferred starting point seems more foundational than any other alternative and would correct the love affair that some materialists have for a third-person point of view.

The importance of beginning with the mental can be highlighted by considering the *disanalogy* of vitalism and consciousness. Dennett rightly points out that vitalism can be critiqued effectively when we focus on the processes (reproduction, metabolism, self-repair) that the vital principle or energy is supposed to explain, but in the case of the mental, thinking, feeling, sensing, and so on are (to use Dennett's analogy) like reproduction, metabolism, and self-repair: the mental is the given, that which we know in first-person direct experience. The mental is not posited or projected but is, rather, a condition for positing or projecting or arguing that, as Dennett suggests, a colleague's interest in consciousness is akin to being interested in cuteness. We can then scientifically discover correlations of the mental and physical, mapping out the neurological conditions enabling persons to function as thinking, acting, feeling beings.

Many years ago, H. H. Farmer stated lucidly the problem with forgetting the first-person perspective:

> If, however, we seek to reflect upon and to grasp the meaning and purpose of the world *as a whole* . . . then clearly this attitude [the setting aside of first-person subjectivity in the name of "objectivity"], normal and proper elsewhere, will not do. Plainly, if we are going to look at and seek to know the world as a whole, we must no longer omit to notice ourselves as looking and knowing; for we, as looking and knowing, and knowing that we are looking and knowing—that is to say as persons—are certainly part of the world *taken as a whole*. The world taken as a whole cannot be merely the world about us; it must be the world which includes us.[36]

If Farmer is correct, then Churchland and Dennett seem bound to elimi-nate what we know as the first person (we may know directly that we are conscious, experiencing selves) because their whole form of inquiry neglects the point of view (experiences) of the inquirer.

The problem with *eliminativism* is that it not only conflicts with what appears to most of us to be the case, but it also seems to undermine its aim: inquiry. Inquiry involves intentional, purposive agency about theo-ries of what exists. There is, in other words, an *aboutness* to inquiry: having inquiry is *about* the world or Shakespeare or whatever. The problem with Rorty's proposal about substituting talk of beliefs with talk of C-fibres is that we still need an account of what the C-fibres are about. Imagine an eliminativist coming up to you and rather than saying, "Please consider whether eliminativism is true," she says, "My C-fibres are firing." No mat-ter how complete and complex the account of the brain, we still need to know what the C-fibres are about, and we might even want to know how the C-fibres and your nervous system make you feel. The eliminativist may propose that we translate the terms "C-fibres firing" into claims such as "Eliminativism is true"—but this does not make it any more plausible that "C-fibres firing" is a thought than if I translate the phrase "I am happy" into "I am miserable," and then conclude that happiness is misery.

We have seen various passages cited earlier in which Dennett seems highly skeptical about conscious experiences. Is he able to sustain this position consistently? I suggest that he is not. In a book critiquing reli-gion, Dennett relates an anecdote in which he seems to fully recognize the primacy of the mental and the understanding of another person (his daughter's) inner subjective states:

> Many years ago, my five-year-old daughter, attempting to imitate the gymnast Nadia Comaneci's performance on the horizontal bar, tipped over the piano stool and painfully crushed two of her fingertips. How was I going to calm down this terrified child so I could safely drive her to the emergency room? Inspiration struck: I held my own hand near her throbbing little hand and sternly ordered: "Look, Andrea! I'm going to teach you a secret! You can push the pain into *my* hand with your mind. Go ahead, *push! Push!*" She tried—and it worked! She'd "pushed the pain"

into Daddy's hand. Her relief (and fascination) were instantaneous. The effect lasted only for minutes, but with a few further administrations of impromptu hypnotic analgesia along the way, I got her to the emergency room, where they could give her the further treatment she needed. . . . I was exploiting her instincts—though the rationale didn't occur to me until years later, when I was reflecting on it.[37]

In another passage in the same book, Dennett seems to be more confident in first-person experiential states than in external, behavioral activity:

When it comes to interpreting religious avowals of others, *everybody is an outsider*. Why? Because religious avowals concern matters that are beyond observation, beyond meaningful test, so the only thing *anybody* can go on is religious behavior, and more specifically, the behavior of *professing*. A child growing up in a culture is like an anthropologist, after all, surrounded by informants whose professing stand in need of interpretation. The fact that your informants are your father and mother, and speak in your mother tongue, does not give you anything more than a slight circumstantial advantage over the adult anthropologist who has to rely on a string of bilingual interpreters to query the informants. (And think about your own case; weren't you ever baffled or confused about just what you were supposed to believe?)[38]

In these two extracts it is hard to suppose that Dennett denies the existence of the self as more than a projection of the brain.

Let me underscore again the difficulty facing Dennett's eliminativism. The problem with his effort to rid us of the mental is further revealed in how he recommends that we ignore the mental as an irreducible reality. In regard to an experiential state such as taste, he says:

What I think you'll find is that you can start elaborating a sort of catalogue of the facts that matter to you at this moment. Maybe it's the particular deliciousness of this taste in my mouth; so what is that deliciousness? Well, I'd like some more, and I can recall it at a later date, and so on. We're going to take care of all that. We're going to include your disposition to want some more, your capacity to recollect, and even the likelihood that you will find yourself pleasurably recollecting this experience of it. There's a huge manifold of reactive dispositions that you're pointing to when you're saying, "This very yumminess right now," and what you have to do is recognize that however indissolvable, however unassailable, however intrinsically present that all seems to you, what has to be explained is that it seems to you, not that it is so.[39]

The problem, though, was noted earlier: if something *seems to you experientially to be the case*, then there is such a thing as *seeming in experience*. John Searle highlights the problem facing those, such as Dennett, who seem to dispense with conscious experience:

> You can't disprove the existence of conscious experiences by proving that they are only an appearance disguising the underlying reality, because *where consciousness is concerned the existence of the appearance is the reality.* If it seems to me exactly as if I am having conscious experiences, then I am having conscious experiences. This is not an epistemic point. I might make various sorts of mistakes about my experiences, for example, if I suffered from phantom limb pains. But whether reliably reported or not, the experience of feeling the pain is identical with the pain in a way that the experience of seeing a sunset is not identical with a sunset.[40]

The stubbornness and foundational nature of the mental is partly revealed in Churchland's and Stich's very statement of their positions. When Churchland writes that "we eventually decided that witches simply do not exist" and Stich refers to early folk theories that we now discover are "screamingly false," they both use mental and what they would call folk language: *deciding* and finding that *beliefs* are false presuppose mental acts and states. It is also difficult to believe that the "folk" ideas of the past, or the majority of them, were "utterly and thoroughly mistaken." Would the "folk" of the past have even survived if they had outrageously false beliefs about their own thinking, needs, desires, and thoroughly false beliefs about the world, past, present, and future? If we had outrageously false beliefs about what is eatable, drinkable, and breathable, we might only live a day or two. I suggest Churchland and Stich have an inflated view of the errors of our ancestors.

Materialist Faith

Consider, in closing, a contemporary materialist, Thomas Nagel who believes that we will one day close the gap between the mental and physical:

> I believe that the explanatory gap in its present form cannot be closed—that so long as we work with our present mental and physical concepts no transparently necessary connection will ever be revealed, between physically described brain processes and sensory experience, of the logical type familiar from the explanation of other natural processes by analysis into their physico-chemical constituents. We have good grounds for believing that the mental supervenes on the physical—i.e. that there is no mental difference without a physical difference. But pure, unexplained supervenience is not a solution but a sign that there is something fundamental we don't know. We cannot regard pure supervenience as the end of the story because that would require the physical to necessitate the mental without there being any answer to the question [of] how it does. But there *must* be a "how," and our task is to understand it. An obviously systematic connection that remains unintelligible to us calls out for a theory.[41]

Nagel does not, however, allow that dualism might provide such a theory—for example, a theory that posits an actual difference between the mental and physical that explains why they appear to be contingently related. He suggests instead that we will eventually come to reconceive the physical world and our mental life in a way that will permit us to recognize that our mental life is part of the physical world and, indeed, essentially so. "I believe," writes Nagel, "it is not irrational to hope that someday, long after we are all dead, people will be able to observe the operation of the brain and say, with true understanding, 'That's what the experience of tasting chocolate looks like from outside.'"[42] According to Nagel, we need a sufficiently expanded understanding of the composition and nature of the physical world so that it can encompass the mental. He proposes that the ideal theory would show us that what we employ mental and physical concepts to refer to, turns out to be the same thing:

> What will be the point of view, so to speak, of such a theory? If we could arrive at it, it would render transparent the relation between mental and physical, not directly, but through the transparency of their common relation to something that is not merely either of them. Neither the mental nor the physical point of view will do because it simply leaves out the physiology, and has no room for it. The physical will not do because while it includes the behavioral and functional manifestations of the mental, this doesn't, in view of the falsity of conceptual reductionism, enable it to reach to the mental concepts themselves. The right point of view would be one which, contrary to present conceptual possibilities, included both subjectivity and spatiotemporal structure from the outset, all its descriptions implying both these things at once, so that it would describe inner states and their functional relations to behavior and to one another from the phenomenological inside and the physiological outside simultaneously—not in parallel.[43]

Nagel's case reveals the difficulty of identifying the mental and physical. We can hope to eventually have a conceptual revolution and perhaps see the mental and physical (as we now see them) as part of some newly conceived, physical thing. But so far, radical materialism seems deeply problematic, and it is not clear, once we acknowledge conscious experience, that we can clearly identify it as a physical phenomenon.

It is too soon to move from this case for beginning our philosophical work with the mental to making sense of the claim that gravity might be a manifestation of love. But I do suggest that eliminative approaches to the mental endanger less extravagant claims, such as: making love can be a manifestation of love. And I will go on to contend in future chapters that the recognition and appreciation of the nature of consciousness can form part of an initial clue, the beginning of a golden cord that can lead us to the divine.

CHAPTER 2

SELVES AND BODIES

> Bless to me my body . . .
> bless to me my soul
> —Gaelic song and blessing

As we have seen in the opening chapter, there is some discord in contemporary philosophical work on consciousness and experience. It is not at all easy to eliminate consciousness from our inquiries nor, once admitted, is it easy to place it in a thoroughgoing physical world. David Chalmers offers this succinct statement of the problem: "You can't have your materialist cake and eat your consciousness too."[1] In the first chapter, I suggested that the reality of consciousness and experience is more evident than the posits of contemporary science. Fortunately or unfortunately, the initial work to prepare for the main focus of this book is not over. A little more work is called for before we can establish a proper foothold to explore Dante's sense that the cosmos is upheld by love, or W. H. Auden's experience of being caught up in the power of love, or the Cambridge Platonist notion of absolute life.

The chair of my philosophy department has a list that appears to be a credo taped to her office door. The list includes: *Naturalism is true.* And: *There are no spooks.* Naturalism is not easy to define. As Barry Stroud observed recently,

> "Naturalism" seems to me in this and other respects rather like "World Peace." Almost everyone swears allegiance to it, and is willing to march under its banner. But disputes still break out about what it is appropriate or acceptable to do in the name of that slogan. And like world peace, once you start specifying concretely exactly what it involves and how to achieve it, it becomes increasingly difficult to reach and to sustain a consistent and exclusive "naturalism."[2]

As hinted at in the introduction, naturalism comes in many forms, and it may or may not take the form of radical materialism. However, the essence of naturalism is the denial that God exists—or even the denial of the possibility of God's existence—and the denial that humans are immaterial or have or contain or are nonphysical souls. To posit God or the soul is far from Stroud's "World Peace"; rather, it is too spooky for naturalists.

This chapter addresses such naturalist concerns about the soul or the self. Is it plausible to think that some version of dualism has a competitive edge in theories of human nature? John Searle, no dualist, comments that today materialism is so entrenched that it is like a religion—something Searle sees as a demerit: "There is a sense in which materialism is the religion of our time, at least among most of the professional experts in the fields of philosophy, psychology, cognitive science, and other disciplines that study the mind. Like more traditional religions, it is accepted without question and it provides the framework within which other questions can be posed, addressed, and answered."[3] I have some evidence that my colleague's credo may treat naturalism as a religion, because at the end of her list of propositions is the word "Amen."

I suggest that we go directly to the mind-body relationship and consider why *tout le monde* thinks dualism is out of bounds. Many philosophers today blame the French philosopher René Descartes for introducing a hideous bifurcation or dualism in which the person (soul or mind) is distinct from his or her body. When I was an undergraduate philosophy major, I was told that Descartes was responsible for almost all contemporary philosophical problems; in my first class I was informed that even the Vietnam War was somehow the fault of Descartes!

Let's look at some of the reasons why Descartes is considered the Prince of Darkness and then see if a somewhat qualified dualism—which may be called *integrative dualism*—has promise. I will fill out "integrative dualism" shortly, but for now I will describe it as the view that the self and body are profoundly integrated but not identical. To summarize what is to follow: After sketching why so many philosophers reject dualism, I argue in this chapter that there is something that my friend and chair would find spooky or odd, given naturalism. Prima facie, there seems to be more to a person than her or his body, and the relationship of person and body seems to be contingent rather than necessary. Strict identity relations appear to be necessary (for example, water is H_2O) but the person-body relationship does not appear to be so. This nonnecessity or contingency does not sit well with standard forms of naturalism and materialism.[4] In chapter 3, I will suggest that we step back to consider consciousness and personal identity in light of theism versus naturalism.

Ghosts in Machines

While Descartes is considered the source of "dualism" in many textbooks, the idea that the self (or soul or mind or person) is not identical with his or her body is far older than the seventeenth century. Plato and Augustine argued against the materialism of their day and, as I hope to show below, some form of dualism seems to be a commonsense (or at least commonplace and natural) position.

One of the most famous attacks on Descartes' dualism in the twentieth century was Gilbert Ryle's book *The Concept of Mind*. Ryle sought to make dualism look like a massive, unnatural severing of the self and body. For him, accepting dualism requires being resigned to the notion that the person is like a ghost in a body that functions like a machine. Ryle developed the following portrait of dualism:

Human bodies are in space and are subject to the mechanical laws which govern all other bodies in space. Bodily processes and states can be inspected by external observers. . . .

But minds are not in space, nor are their operations subject to mechanical laws. The workings of one mind are not witnessable by other observers; its career is private. Only I can take direct cognizance of the states and processes of my own mind. A person therefore lives through two collateral histories, one consisting of what happens in and to his body, the other consisting of what happens in and to his mind. The first is public, the second is private. . . .

It has been disputed whether a person does or can directly monitor all or only some of the episodes of his own private history; but, according to the official doctrine, of at least some of these episodes he has direct and unchallengeable cognizance. . . . He may have great or small uncertainties about concurrent and adjacent episodes in the physical world, but he can have none about at least part of what is momentarily occupying his mind.[5]

Ryle further contends that this general, disjointed configuration (or really, disfiguration) of human nature is what Descartes offered us in the seventeenth century. He elaborates on this model:

Material objects are situated in a common field, known as 'space', and what happens to one body in one part of space is mechanically connected with what happens to other bodies in other parts of space. But mental happenings occur in insulated fields, known as 'minds', and there is, apart maybe from telepathy no direct causal connection between what happens in one mind and what happens in another. Only through the medium of the public physical world can the mind of one person make a difference to the mind of another. The mind is its own place and in his inner life each of us lives the life of a ghostly Robinson Crusoe. People can see, hear and jolt one another's bodies, but they are irremediably blind and deaf to the workings of one another's mind and inoperative upon them. . . .

As thus represented, minds are not merely ghosts harnessed to machines, they are themselves just spectral machines. Though the human body is an engine, it is not quite an ordinary engine, since some of its workings are governed by another engine inside it—this interior governor-engine being one of a very special sort. It is invisible, inaudible and it has no size or weight. It cannot be taken to bits and the laws it obeys are not those known to ordinary engineers. Nothing is known of how it governs the bodily engine.[6]

Ryle's critique is complemented by many other philosophers who contend that dualism provides us with an absurd portrait of the mind-body relationship. According to Antony Flew, dualists wind up treating the body as a container. And yet, argues Flew, don't we see other people in our normal interactions, not their containers? Peter Hacker and Anthony Kenny liken dualism to the thesis that a person is like a tiny invisible character operating somewhere in or around the brain.

Trenton Merricks has a simple argument against dualism. He can kiss and has kissed his wife. Merricks argues that if dualism is true, then he has only kissed her body. Perhaps, if he is right and dualism is true, then souls cannot kiss or hold hands or go for walks, and so on. He appears to suppose that, for dualists, kissing involves a soul getting its body to make the appropriate move. And insofar as we all know that kissing is an intimate, proximate action, we all have grounds for rejecting dualism.

The most important charge against dualism has been noted in chapter 1 but not yet fully addressed. If dualism is true, then how does one account for the causal interaction of a nonphysical, nonspatial mind with a physical, spatial body? Daniel Dennett thinks that the problem of this mysterious interaction of mental and physical makes dualism antiscientific and unacceptable: "This fundamentally anti-scientific stance of dualism is, to my mind, its most disqualifying feature, and is the reason why in this book I adopt the apparently dogmatic rule that dualism is to be avoided *at all costs*. It is not that I think I can give a knock-down proof that dualism, in all its forms, is false or incoherent, but that, given the way dualism wallows in mystery, *accepting dualism is giving up*."[7] Dennett appears to be claiming that dualism is out of bounds because it winds up positing a scientifically inscrutable causal relation. The causal link between mental states and physical states seems to go beyond the kind of scientific inquiries one undertakes in physics, chemistry, and biology.

A Conversation about Dualism

The contemporary conversation about dualism requires a few interruptions. The first is very modest. The word "dualism" is profoundly unhelpful in the current debate. It was coined first to describe the Zoroastrianism belief that there are two chief cosmic forces—a good and an evil God. None of those canonical philosophers in the past who distinguished the soul (or mind or person) from the body employed "dualism" to describe their positions (Plato, Augustine, Descartes, Locke). I strongly suspect that this past usage, in which "dualism" names a duality of good and evil, still haunts us and explains why so many people think that if you are a dualist, then you value the mind and denigrate or treat the body as evil or bad. Indeed, many theologians write as though dualism is the equivalent of patriarchy, anti-ecology, economism, and other similarly anti-body notions.[8] But, as I shall note briefly, there is no reason whatever to link integrative dualism with this body hatred.

Second, and this may be one reason why philosophers Plato, Augustine, or Descartes did not employ the term "dualism," so-called dualists would be more accurately described as opponents of *monism* (one-ism; in this case they are opposed to thinking that the person is only her body) or proponents of *pluralism* (the idea that there is more than one kind of thing). Dualists did not develop their position historically by first positing two kinds of things—the physical and the nonphysical—and then asking which kind of thing is the self or consciousness. Rather, it was argued by Descartes and Plato and others that we have some knowledge of the self (or soul or mind), and when we consider whether the self is identical with the body, we have some reason to think that the answer is no. A person is *more* than her or his body, or at least the body as described by the materialist of the ancient and modern worlds.

Third, one needs to appreciate that while so-called dualists can recognize cases in which a person is like a ghost in a machine, they also recognize that in the case of healthy, integrated embodiment, *a person functions as a unity*. Unless I am paralyzed or I have lost motor and cognitive control over my body, then to see me in action is to see me. But, severe brain damage may leave me utterly paralyzed and with the feeling that my body is a mere container. And perhaps severe psychological disintegration could leave me in the position described by Ryle.

Consider the following: Imagine that I harbor, but never express, deeply vile emotions. Never. In that case, everyone might think me cheerful, but this is indeed only a "public affair" and not something I ever express with angry words or gestures. My malice and its history would, then, be private episodes or a matter of mental operations. I may be so severed from my physical, public persona that my malice is given no visibility (gestures), audition (angry words), and, in a sense, no size or weight. I would actually be in the bifurcated state that Ryle caricatures. We can easily make sense of such a breakdown in terms of Merrick's example. You believe, for example, that you are kissing the love of your life when in actuality you are kissing someone who is only interested in your disposable income.

Integrating Person and Body

Let's now consider *integrative dualism*. Some dualists do (alas) foster a somewhat bifurcated mind-body relationship. Presumably you do not harbor vile emotions that are never expressed. Hopefully, the person you are romantically involved with actually cares about you, and vice versa, so that when you kiss, you offer tactile signs of the reality of embodied love. Those whom I am calling *integrative dualists* deny that there is a strict identity of person and body (as in: water *is* H$_2$O), but at the same time they affirm the profound interwoven unity that constitutes an embodied person when such embodiment is, indeed, healthy and functional.[9]

So, the first point is that integrated dualism does not lead to the absurdities of Ryle's caricature. Under absurd or tragic conditions, his description may match reality, but under healthy, normal conditions Ryle's ghost story is wide of the mark. I suggest that it is Dennett who has turned the self into a ghost, for it is no more real (on his account) than the idea of a center of gravity, a useful reference point but an abstraction and not itself a substantial individual.

The integrative dualist account of persons sees us as fully embodied. On this view, the account is not at all like Richard Taylor's illustration in his book *Metaphysics*, in which a duck (representing a human) is pictured with a sketchy duck floating above it.[10] Perhaps the integrative and materialist position should be pictured as an ambiguous unity, the way the famous duck-rabbit figure is represented. This is a figure that may appear as a duck or a rabbit depending on the angle from which it is viewed. As other philosophers have remarked, if faced with something that could be either a duck or rabbit, run toward it and, if it flies away, conclude that it is a duck, whereas if it hops away, chances are that it is a rabbit. I suggest a similar point with integrative dualism, where one sees a healthy human person as a functional unity. The additional claim is that if you reflect further, philosophically, you can find reasons for a nonidentity between the mental and physical, and thus reasons for adopting integrative dualism rather than physicalism.

And now what of the problem of causal interaction? I suggest that this is not a problem, or no less of a mystery, given integrative dualism than it is for any plausible account of materialism. Consider four points. First, integrative dualists may see the self as spatial, not only in the sense that in a healthy embodiment, persons embody and express their authentic selves, but also in the sense that selves are spatially extended. I feel myself as spread out in space. In a healthy embodiment, my phenomenal (felt) body is coincident with my physical body. This can be ruptured in trauma—I might lose an arm and yet have a phantom limb; an experience of my limb as still intact. If this view is correct, then mind-body interaction is not a case of the nonspatial interacting with what is spatial.

Second, contra Dennett and Churchland, appealing to the law of the conservation of energy causes no greater problem for dualists than it does for materialists. The law of the conservation of energy states that the amount of energy in a closed system must remain constant. It does not specify what kind of energy is involved, nor does the law govern how energy is distributed. As David Rosenthal writes, "The dualist need not adopt the unintuitive idea that mental events never cause bodily events. Conservation of energy dictates only that the energy in a closed physical system is constant, not also how that energy is distributed within the system. Since mental events could effect bodily changes by altering that distribution of energy, the conservation principle does not preclude minds' having bodily effects."[11] Moreover, if a philosopher assumes from the outset that all causation can only be *physical causation*, then the philosopher is simply begging the question against the advocate of integrative dualism.

Further, so long as materialists allow that persons think and reason, they have to allow that such causation does not violate the conservation law. Yet, thinking and reasoning are mental operations. In the activity of reasoning, we come to accept conclusions on the basis of the logical and evident links between beliefs. So, when contemplating which number is the smallest perfect number (a number that is equal to the sum of its divisors, including 1, but not including itself), one reaches the conclusion "6" by reasoning that 6 is equal to 2 + 3 + 1; there is no lower number that fulfills the condition of being a perfect number. If materialists think that human bodies can reason, then what is the problem with integrative dualists who claim that such reasoning involves selves who are embodied and yet are more than the chemical-physical processes involved? The materialist will maintain that they do not have an interaction between the physical and nonphysical (for them, thinking is a brain activity), but they still need to preserve thinking as a mental operation involving reason. And if they allow that that operation doesn't violate energy conservation, then why would a dualist account of mental activity violate it? If a naturalist goes so far as to deny mental causation in the form of reasoning (where a person's thinking of x supports or gives evidence for her to think y is true), then such a naturalism undermines reasoning itself, including the kind of reasoning that supports naturalism.[12]

Third, almost all forms of materialism allow that at a fundamental level there are brute, not further explainable, causal powers. We can explain the property of macroscopic objects and processes in terms of microprocesses, but can this explanation continue without end? Many think that you must get to objects or particles with basic properties to avoid an infinite regress. An infinite regress of explanations would leave us without an account of why there is any causation at all. Thus, if you can have physical objects with basic powers, why not nonphysical beings? Dennett's complaint that dualism leads to mystery and is thus antiscientific rests on a false premise: positing basic, not further explainable, causal powers is not necessarily antiscientific, nor is it antiscientific if we recognize irreducible kinds of things.[13]

Fourth, Churchland and others fail to appreciate the way in which dualists—in particular, integrative dualists—can recognize the profound interrelationship of the mental and the physical. In *Matter and Consciousness*, Churchland writes:

> If there really is a distinct entity in which reasoning, emotion, and consciousness take place, and if that entity is dependent on the brain for nothing more than sensory experiences as input and volitional executions as output, *then one would expect reason, emotion, and consciousness to be relatively invulnerable to direct control or pathology by manipulation or damage to the brain.* But in fact the exact opposite is true. Alcohol, narcotics, or senile degeneration of nerve tissue will impair, cripple, or even destroy one's capacity for rational thought. Psychiatry knows of hundreds of emotion-controlling chemicals (lithium, chloropromazine, amphetamine, cocaine, and so on) that do their work when vectored into the brain. And the vulnerability of consciousness to anesthetics, to caffeine, and to something as simple as a sharp blow to the head shows its very close dependence on neural activity in the brain. All of this makes perfect sense if reason, emotion, and consciousness are activities of the brain itself. But it makes very little sense if they are activities of something else entirely [emphasis mine].[14]

I find Churchland's point unconvincing. No contemporary dualists deny tight interconnections between the mental and the physical. To portray dualists as holding the mind or person as "something else entirely" from the body explicitly denies the dualist thesis that human persons are indeed embodied. The idea that a dualist would deny the fact that alcohol affects the mind recalls a lecture I once heard at New York University in which a philosopher claimed that students can disprove dualism by drinking excessive amounts of alcohol and then observing the results. In reply to Churchland, I suggest that we can only make sense of the dual nature of alcohol consumption, both its physical and mental components—from a moderate glass of wine over discussions of Dante to the unhealthy craving that causes brain and liver damage and loss of consciousness—if we believe that more is involved than physical-chemical processes. Churchland's point can also be reversed: the fact that reason, emotion, and consciousness impact our physiology and behavior makes little sense if all we have doing the causal work is brain activity.

Further points can be made in reply to the interaction problem. For example, objecting to integrative dualism by an appeal to the principle of the conservation of energy is embarrassed by the fact that the principle does not apply to all physical interactions, as seen in general relativity theory. As the physicist Robert Wald observes, "In general relativity there exists no meaningful expression for gravitational stress-energy and thus there is no meaningful local energy conservation law which leads to a statement of energy conservation."[15] The contemporary view of the physical is, arguably, too fluid now for materialists to confidently think that they can (as Dennett does) rule out dualist interaction in principle.

Having canvassed reasons for rejecting integrative dualism and found them wanting, why adopt integrative dualism?

Some Positive Reasons for Integrated Dualism

There are many reasons for not being swayed by contemporary forms of materialistic naturalism and opting instead for integrative dualism. But first, a little background: If a person *is* her body, then anything true of the person must be true of her body. This is a feature of what philosophers call the *indiscernability of identicals*, as noted in chapter 1. Consider again any two pairings in which two names are used to refer to the same thing: Morning Star and Evening Star, Mark Twain and Samuel Clemens, Cassius Clay and Muhammad Ali, and so on. Assuming that each of these refers, strictly speaking, to the same thing, then anything that is true of one is true of the other. To box with Muhammad Ali is to box with Cassius Clay. Given this principle, it appears that some things are true of persons, but not true of their bodies, and thus there is a reason for holding that persons are not their bodies. Consider just three areas.

Disembodiment and Bodies without Selves

If the self is her or his body, then the self cannot exist without her or his body, and vice versa. Take, however, the possibility of disembodiment. W. D. Hart offers this thought experiment:

> Imagine that, still embodied, you wake up tomorrow in your bed. Before raising your eyelids, you stumble over to a mirror in your room. Pointing your face at the mirror, you now raise your eyelids. What you see in the mirror is that your eye sockets are empty. . . .
>
> Curious. So you probe the empty sockets with your little finger. You can imagine how they would feel, and how the empty channel where the optic nerve once lay would feel. Interesting. So you saw off the top of your skull with your surgical saw and, lo and behold, your skull is empty. . . .
>
> You've imagined what seems to be seeing without the two bodily or-gans, eyes and a brain, [that] most people think are essential to seeing. You don't need your legs to see, so imagine them away. You don't need your arms to see, so imagine them away. You don't need your trunk to see, so imagine it away. You don't need the rest of your head to see, so imagine it away. Now your whole body is gone, but *you* are still there seeing what is reflected in the mirror. Of course that is no longer your face or any of your body; it is probably just the wall behind you.[16]

Richard Swinburne, too, envisions what it might be like to become dis-embodied. If a person can exist without his body, even if it never happens, then a body cannot exist in a disembodied state:

> Imagine yourself . . . gradually ceasing to be affected by alcohol or drugs, your thinking being too equally coherent however men mess about with your brain. Imagine too that you cease to feel any pains, aches, and thrills, although you remain aware of what is going on in what has been called your body. You gradually find yourself aware of what is going on in bodies other than your own and other material objects at any place in space—at any rate to the extent of being able to give invariably true answers to questions about these things, an ability which proves unaffected by men

interfering with lines of communication, e.g., turning off lights so that agents which rely on sight cannot see, shutting things in rooms so that agents which rely on hands to feel things cannot do so. You also come to see things from any point of view which you choose, possibly simultaneously, possibly not. You remain able to talk and wave your hands about, but find yourself able to move anything which you choose, including the hands of other people.[17]

Here, Swinburne is seeking to fill out an experiential picture of divine powers. He is imaginatively sketching what it would be like to have causal properties extend beyond one's body.[18]

In fact, there is an impressive collection of literature in which persons report out-of-body experiences (OBEs) when they are near death or have even been pronounced dead prior to resuscitation. Let's assume that all such experiences are not accurate accounts of persons actually leaving their bodies. But even granting that the experiences are false or unreliable, don't they at least appear to describe a coherent, bona fide possibility? If we have reason to think that a person can (even if she never does) survive the annihilation of her body, then there is something true of her, but not true of her body.

Some of the criticism of Swinburne's thought experiment are not, in my view, compelling. Peter van Inwagen objects:

> I can't imagine any of this. I can't even imagine myself ceasing to be affected by alcohol, in any sense that will help Swinburne. I can, of course, imagine my never drinking any alcohol and thus "ceasing to be affected" by it; but clearly that isn't what Swinburne has in mind. Or I can (perhaps) imagine myself drinking alcohol that is removed from my system by Martians before it reaches my brain; but this gets us no forwarder. . . . Can I imagine alcohol having its usual effects on my brain but no effect on my sobriety? I can't, and I am sure that anyone who thinks he can "imagine" these things has just not thought the matter through.[19]

But contemporary neurology and philosophy have not yet shown there to be a *necessary* connection between brain states and mental states. We do not yet have an account of why certain brain states produce certain mental states. By way of a further reply to van Inwagen, it seems that we can imagine the body as it is and yet the person has ceased to be. Consider the case in which a person falls into a deep coma. She as a person has ceased to be, despite the fact that the bodily organs continue to function.

Van Inwagen has also objected to arguments involving thought experiments on the grounds of a general skepticism about the imagination. Our imagination can deceive us. Perhaps I only appear to be able to be disembodied, but this is not a bona fide possibility. In reply, I suggest that we should be careful in appealing to the imagination as an infallible guide to recognizing what is and is not possible. Someone might imagine in vivid terms time travel (for example, *Back to the Future*), and yet it is impossible. (Perhaps time is necessarily one-directional.) Still, if you carefully consider some state of affairs and you can envision or describe it as actual, and it does not conflict with anything you know to be necessary, then you have reason to believe that it is possible. I suggest that we can envisage disembodiment (and other states of affairs to be noted); it does not conflict with any independently known, necessary truths, and thus it is reasonable to believe it to be possible.[20]

One more point about disembodiment: I should add that Swinburne's and Hart's thought experiments may describe what it might be like to survive the death of one's body, but they are not ipso facto descriptions of something we may readily see as good. That is, while it may be good to die to be with "the Lord" (more on this later), the loss of one's body can be seen by integrative dualists as a deep injury or profound severance. Hart's story, for example, may well strike us as horrifying. Perhaps this horror is fitting; perhaps we should find disembodiment chilling. The coherence of such an event should cause us dismay. Integrative dualism is well positioned to see embodiment as good and its loss as bad. Consider a different case in which something is true of a person but not true of her body.

Body-Switching

If you are indeed your body, then you could not switch bodies or have yours replaced and remain the same. However, we seem to be able to grasp what it would be like to have a different body, different gender, and so on. Millions (perhaps just under 1.5 billion) of Hindus and Buddhists believe in reincarnation, in which a soul comes to have a new body; it may be hard to prove that reincarnation occurs but more difficult to know that reincarnation is impossible. Arguably, imagining that one might switch bodies with persons seems in part to be what we picture when we truly empathize with another person or carry out the Golden Rule. A person might be perfectly reasonable in asking you whether your views on famine relief, abortion, and so on would change if you had been born in poverty or had lived a very different sort of life or were of a different gender or ethnicity.

Some objections to the possibility of body-switching actually seem to underestimate our moral imagination. Consider this example from Bernard Williams:

> Suppose a magician is hired to perform the old trick of making the emperor and the peasant become each other. He gets the emperor and the peasant in one room, with the emperor on his throne and the peasant in the corner, and then casts the spell. What will count as success? Clearly . . . the emperor's body, with the peasant's personality, should be on the throne, and the peasant's body with the emperor's personality, in the corner. What does this mean? In particular, what has happened to the voices? The voice presumably ought to count as a bodily function; yet how would the peasant's gruff blasphemies be uttered in the emperor's cultivated tones, or the emperor's witticisms in the peasant's growl? A similar point holds for the features; the emperor's body might include the sort of face that just could not express the peasant's morose suspiciousness, the peasant's face a face no expression of which could be taken for one of fastidious arrogance. These "could"s are not just empirical—such expressions on these features might be unthinkable.[21]

But doesn't this objection overlook the fact that class distinctions are not necessary? When the emperor realizes that, after all, he could have been a peasant and the peasant realizes that he might have been an emperor, the first step is taken toward the possibility of change. Are we really to believe that a peasant is necessarily given over to gruff blasphemies and the emperor is essentially witty and cultivated? These sorts of conditions seem contingent, not essential. If so, we have a further reason for not identifying the person and the body.

Williams and others may object that if the person can be detached or severed and switch bodies, then we run the risk of undermining the real foundation for personal identity over time: bodily continuity. The problem with insisting on bodily continuity, however, is that it does not seem to be essential (as observed in the next argument). But more important, bodily continuity is deemed vital because of psychological or personal continuity. Novels like such as Woolf's *To the Lighthouse* demonstrate how personal identity may be compellingly portrayed by following the different streams of consciousness of the characters. Woolf is brilliant at moving the readers from person to person as she shifts the mood and perspectives in the thoroughly psychological landscape. The physical world is not at all ignored (there is the house, the lighthouse, and so on) but, rather, bathed in psychological designs, projects, conflicts, anticipation, and other emotions.

Personal Identity over Time

This argument is related to the previous one but is slightly different. We have evidence that every seven years your body is almost completely replaced by new cells. Your body is not the same as the one you had in, say, kindergarten, but, at least in accord with common sense, you are the same person. If so, we have reason to think that you are not identical with your body. In a thought experiment, we can imagine that over time every part is replaced, and thus at the end of this gradual replacement (say, after ten years) it is not the same body you had before. Nonetheless we can imagine that you remain the same person.[22]

Loving Selves and Bodies

Let me bring this back to the topic of love. What is it to love another person? I suggest that it is to desire and take pleasure in her flourishing. This is something I return to in chapter 7, but it is fitting to sketch the following line of reasoning here. Sadly, it appears that our bodies have a natural terminus, a point at which they wear out. But do we think that there is a natural time when a person has a terminus or ending? Insofar as we identify the person with her body, it might be reasonable to think so. And yet at the death of someone (no matter how old) whom you love deeply, it is difficult to believe that the value or worth of a person has been exhausted or has reached a natural ending. Our concept of *being a person* at least appears to be that of a man or woman who is capable of unending growth, love, learning, and relationships. If this line of reasoning has any purchase with you, then you have some basis for thinking that the concept of the good of a person transcends or goes beyond the good of her body. While this line of reasoning recognizes a goodness about persons (their inexhaustible value) not possessed by bodies, this implies no denigration of the body. In a healthy state, to love a person will be *embodied* insofar as one cares for the whole of a person. And yet we can appreciate this, while also appreciating that there is a good to persons who can, if there is a God who preserves us in being, outlast the good of the body.

I suggest that further reflection on what it is to love provides a bit more evidence for the intuitive plausibility of integrative dualism. For those naturalists who acknowledge that there is conscious experience and so on, human persons are identical with their bodies. *You* are the same thing as your body now. On this view, however, you *as a person* are a *mode* or *way that your body is* rather than a substantial individual. Arguably, your body existed before you did as a conscious being (in your first days as a fetus), and your body will probably survive (as a corpse) after you, the person, dies. In this sense, then, you as a person are *a phase* or *period* that your body undergoes. Phases or modes can be of different degrees of value and lengths (say, being a boy or girl versus the phase of manhood or womanhood). But when it comes to persons, don't we experience ourselves as substantial individuals who can love and are loved as individuals? In loving my wife, for example, am I loving a phase or period that her animal body is passing through? I don't think so! Romantic love and the experience of someone's death mark occasions when we are vividly aware of the substantial individual identity of persons.

When I was present at a dear one's death, I experienced the loss of the person as an *individual.* The body was still in the room; the breathing had stopped. If some forms of materialism are true (you are your body), then the person stage has elapsed but you might still be there (if the body remains intact), but this seems quite contrary to our ordinary experience and beliefs.

Søren Kierkegaard seemed to deeply appreciate how love manages to focus and hold on to the beloved in a way that is everlasting and enduring. In *Works of Love*, he points out:

> The beloved can treat you in such a way that he is lost to you, and you can lose a friend, but whatever a neighbour does to you, you can never lose him. To be sure, you can also continue to love your beloved and your friend no matter how they treat you, but you cannot truthfully continue to call them beloved and friend when they, sorry to say, have really changed. No change, however, can take your neighbour from you, for it is not your neighbour who holds you fast—it is your love which holds your neighbour fast.[23]

In loving another person deeply, we may become ever more appreciative of his or her precious, irreplaceable individuality. Insofar as this is an authentic grasp of who the beloved is, we have reason to doubt that a person is a mode or phase of something else, such as her animal body.[24]

Ghosts in Machines Revisited

Before examining theism and naturalism further as "big pictures" or comprehensive philosophies, let's reconsider Ryle's project. In the lengthy passage cited earlier and throughout his book *The Concept of Mind*, Ryle implies that the dualist invents a kind of shadow world, a realm that is cut off from the main evident realm of spatial objects and public causal interactions. I want to stress a slightly different point: people vary in their values, interests, and passions so significantly that they may be said to be in different worlds. It is commonplace to distinguish different worlds from a social point of view: there are the worlds of sports, art, fashion, and so on. In a sense, how you conceive and value yourself and those around you can give rise to very different worlds. For Hemingway, for example, the world he sees may allow for love, but it is dominated by chance, rivalry, drinking, sex, grim and seemingly purposeless conflict, brief and sometimes brilliant alliances, and death (in *A Farewell to Arms,* Frederic Henry and Catherine Barkley love each other, but their affair is cut short).

The Cambridge Platonists deeply appreciated how our inner mental virtues or vices can give rise to very different worlds or places. Benjamin Whichcote advanced this thesis in an aphorism: "Heaven is *first* a Temper, *then* a Place."[25] If you approach the world with the love of the good and the true and the beautiful, Whichcote proposed, then you bring heaven, or you begin to bring a little heaven into being. This concept of how the inner can shape the outer, public world was later given expression in John Milton's *Paradise Lost,* when he records Satan's boast: "The mind is its own place, and in itself / Can make a Heav'n of Hell, a Hell of Heav'n."[26]

In closing, then, I suggest that there is some value in seeing the world and life itself as a mix of the inner and outer, the mental and the physical. The key point of integrative dualism is that we can avoid seeing the person in thoroughly ethereal, spectral terms (as a spook), and we can also realize that the observable world is an arena in which we can experience and act on our inner thoughts and desires.

CHAPTER 3

SOME BIG PICTURES

One need only shut oneself in a closet and begin to
think of the fact of one's being there, of one's queer
bodily shape in the darkness . . . of one's fantastic
character and all, to have the wonder steal over the
detail as much as over the general fact of being, and
to see that it is only familiarity that blunts it.

—William James

At the beginning of this book I introduced a school of philosophers,
the Cambridge Platonists, who in the seventeenth century advanced the
Christian faith with a supreme focus on the good, the true, and the beautiful. For them, an experiential grasp of divine love animates and expands
one's love of nature. In *A Discourse of the Freedom of the Will,* Peter Sterry
writes: "If God is love, his work is the work of love, of a love unmixed,
unconfined, supreme, infinite in wisdom and power, not limited in its
workings by any preexistent matter, but bringing forth freely and entirely
from itself its whole work both matter and form, according to its own

inclination and complacency in itself."[1] Sterry and the other Cambridge Platonists defended this vision of temporal and eternal love—they would have agreed with Dante that gravity and all celestial and terrestrial reality is the result of God's creative love—over against the Daniel Dennett of their day, Thomas Hobbes.[2] As noted in the last chapter, this rich, expansive portrait of love does not, however, meet with enthusiasm among a host of naturalists. From the standpoint of secular naturalism, the Platonic Christian view of God and the good should be disparaged as mere fable and superstition because of its lack of scientific credibility. Without taking on the big pictures of naturalism, I find that the debate over religious experience is seriously curtailed.

I vividly saw the need to look at background assumptions in an exchange I had with coauthor Stewart Goetz and naturalist Matthew Bagger at an American Academy of Religion meeting. Bagger was assigned the task of critiquing *Naturalism*, a book written by Goetz and me that is highly critical of naturalism and raises some objections to Bagger's own work. There was an extraordinary, bizarre book launch at a San Diego cocktail lounge complete with bouncers and blaring disco music; and pages of our book (along with a few other books that were part of the launch) were projected on a screen above the bar, where the bartender was mixing drinks with hard liquor. As muddled as that evening turned out to be, it became evident in our exchange with Bagger that only a critical challenge to naturalism could open the door to the possibility of theistic religious experience. Without considering which of these big pictures of reality may be true, the credibility or incredibility of religious experience cannot be productively examined. Bagger maintained—as he puts it in his *Religious Experience, Justification, and History*—that it is now unacceptable to appeal to "a transcendent order of reality (and causation) distinct from the mundane order presupposed alike by the natural scientist and the rest of us in our quotidian affairs."[3] While Goetz and I, like the Cambridge Platonists, think that a transcendent order may in fact be experienced under ordinary and extraordinary conditions, Bagger's position is nonetheless consistent and lucid: "Our naturalism constitutes grounds for rejecting epistemological theories which permit supernatural explanation."[4]

In this chapter, let us consider, under less intoxicating and noisy conditions, the naturalist critique and whether it utterly undermines the idea that the loves and goods of this world can be hints of an eternal God.

The Incoherence of Theism

Some naturalists charge that theism is utterly incoherent: it makes no sense or, putting the matter succinctly, it is nonsense. For many decades the Canadian philosopher Kai Nielsen has argued that theism is incoherent.

> We are no better off with the stars in the heavens spelling out GOD EXISTS than with their spelling out PROCRASTINATION DRINKS MELANCHOLY. We know that something has shaken our world, but we know not what; we know—or think that we know, how could we tell which it was in such a circumstance? —that we heard a voice coming out of the sky and we know—or again think that we know—that the stars rearranged themselves right before our eyes and on several occasions to spell out that GOD EXISTS. But are we wiser by observing this about what "god" refers to or what a pure disembodied spirit transcendent to the universe is or could be? At most we might think that maybe those religious people have something—something we know not what—going for them. But we also might think it was some kind of big trick or some mass delusion. The point is that we wouldn't know what to think.[5]

For Nielsen, theism as a hypothesis is like Chomsky's famous case of nonsense that philosophers like to quote (as noted in chapter 1), "Colorless green ideas sleep furiously." Theism posits a being who exists beyond the universe. In Nielsen's views, this is positing a being beyond sense or beyond what can be meaningfully referenced.

In *Christianity and Paradox*, Ronald Hepburn claims that theism faces a deep, logical problem. It is impossible, in his view, to think or describe a being that is beyond or outside the cosmos:

Why *not* imagine a being entirely outside the universe, infusing energy *into* the universe, without becoming in any way part of it? Why is this absurd? It is absurd because in imagining this, we inevitably picture the world as a limited system with a boundary beyond which dwells the God who is the world's cause. But this would really be no different from thinking of a *part* of the world and of a being who dwells in *another* part but is in contact with the first.[6]

If Hepburn is right, it makes no sense for there to be an extra-universe or cosmic creator. And Gareth Moore similarly lampoons the idea of God as an invisible spirit:

We say that God is invisible, intangible etc. These traditional attributes of God have their part to play in theology and in the spiritual life of Christians. Treating the existence of God as a hypothesis makes them look like makeshifts for the purpose of preserving the hypothesis from falsification, as if they said, "God is there all right, as the evidence indicates, but the reason you can't discover him is that he is invisible, etc., and not accessible to your sense or detectable by your instruments." But that cast-iron defense of the "hypothesis" only serves to make it idle, a kind of joke, like saying, "there is a green, three-legged, ten-foot-tall woman in the middle of the road, only you can't detect her because she is invisible, intangible, etc." And one would still be left with the problem [of] why any phenomena could be understood as evidence for this hypothesis.[7]

Moore instead thinks that religious beliefs should not be treated as claims about a reality that we can test and debate intelligently. Although not Moore's analogy, the belief that there is an invisible, intangible, odorless, undetectable cat in a room would not be dislodged if one claimed that no such cat is seen, touched, smelled, or detected. A believer in such a cat might reply to a skeptic: "Of course you cannot see it. The cat is *invisible*. If you could see the cat, it wouldn't be invisible." But then one would need to know why anyone would believe in such a cat in the first place. Theism is in a similar fix, according to Moore.

Jan Narveson, like Moore and Nielsen, argues that theism as a hypothesis is an impoverished worldview, for it lacks any explanatory power. Narveson proposes that contemporary theists are not better off than those holding to an anthropomorphic mythology:

> It ought to be regarded as a major embarrassment to natural theology that the very idea of something like a universe's being "created" by some minded being is sufficiently mind-boggling that any attempt to provide a detailed account of how it might be done is bound to look silly, or mythical, or a vaguely anthropomorphized version of some familiar physical process. Creation stories abound in human societies, as we know. Accounts ascribe the creation to various mythical beings, chief gods among a sizeable polytheistic committee, giant tortoises, super-mom hens, and, one is tempted to say, God-knows-what. The Judeo-Christian account does no better, and perhaps does a bit worse, in proposing a "six-day" process of creation.[8]

Narveson further holds that theism is defective because it is unable to explain how it is that divine agency functions:

> It is plainly no surprise that details about just *how* all this was supposed to have happened [God creating the cosmos] are totally lacking when they are not, as I say, silly or simply poetic. For the fundamental idea is that some infinitely powerful mind simply willed it to be thus, and as they say, Lo!, it was so! If we aren't ready to accept that as an explanatory description—as we should not be, since it plainly doesn't *explain* anything, as distinct from merely asserting that it was in fact done—then where do we go from there? . . . "How are we supposed to know the ways of the infinite and almighty God?" it is asked—as if that put-down made a decent substitute for an answer. But of course it doesn't. If we are serious about "natural theology," then we ought to be ready to supply content in our explication of theological hypotheses. . . . An explanation's right to be called "scientific" is, indeed, in considerable part earned precisely by its ability to provide such detail.[9]

Narveson concludes that theism is to be rejected due to its profoundly unscientific or antiscientific philosophy.

These sorts of arguments appeal to what might be called the big picture. In Narveson's view, explanations in terms of dualism or theism appear lame compared to scientific materialism. Brian O'Shaughnessy comments on the comparative strength of an appeal to scientific causes versus the appeal to divine agency: "Four centuries of triumphant advance by the rock-bottom physical science of physics cannot but leave some mark on philosophy. When you can predict the wave length of a spectrum line to eight decimal places it is rather more difficult to believe that the underlying reality of everything is spiritual, e.g., an immaterial deity. After all, should a deity be so fastidious?"[10]

Objections were raised against some forms of materialism in chapters 1 and 2, but some philosophers hold that even if materialistic naturalism has some trouble accounting for consciousness and selves, this would not be a sufficient reason to abandon materialistic naturalism. As Leopold Studenberg observes, "Materialistic science stands unrivaled. The belief that consciousness will force this giant onto its knees may even seem slightly mad."[11] Colin McGinn similarly notes that naturalism is currently judged to have far greater support than theism. From the point of view of naturalism, a theistic account of consciousness looks like a miracle or a parlor trick, and, faced with such an option, we should always opt for naturalism: "One wants to insist consciousness cannot *really* be miraculous, some kind of divine parlor trick. It must fit into the natural order of things somehow. Its relation to matter must be intelligible, principled, law-governed. Naturalism about consciousness is not merely an option. It is a condition of understanding. It is a condition of existing."[12]

Some naturalists, such as David Hume, make a further point. The existence of the observed spatiotemporal universe is unique. We can make sense of a host of galaxies, but, according to some naturalists, not a host of universes. In our unique universe, we are simply unable to reason about whether there is a creative designing intelligence "behind" it or at its origin, assuming that it has an origin. If universes were plentiful and we had a way of telling which ones were created, fine; but they aren't, so we cannot compare and contrast universes in the way that we might compare and contrast islands and then question whether they have been created or are inhabited.

Richard Dawkins claims to be virtually certain that there is no God, and it is worth finishing up this sample of naturalist critiques by considering his argument. His overall thesis is advanced as a scientific precept: the complexity of a being (reality or event) is explained in terms of the simple—simpler beings or events. So, in accounting for glaciers, forests, human beings, frogs, planets, the explanation is to be carried out by an appeal to simpler and simpler forces. As a thesis within biology or physics, this seems reasonable. Dawkins then argues that God, if there is a God, must be highly complex—indeed, no less complex than the cosmos that, according to theists, God creates and sustains: "A God capable of continuously monitoring and controlling the individual status of every particle in the universe *cannot* be simple."[13] Then God, as a being, must be explained by something simpler. But unless one posits simpler gods from whom God evolved (and this would be preposterous), theism should be rejected.

The Incoherence of the Incoherence

The above barrage of objections is forceful, but we are compelled to step back and survey theism on its own terms.[14] Unless we assume from the beginning that naturalism is the *only* alternative, we need to consider the decisive dividing point between theism and naturalism. Theism contends that the most fundamental reality in the cosmos is an all-good, necessarily existing, intentional reality. According to theism, the cosmos is sustained by a teleological, purposive being that is noncontingent: that is, God does not exist accidentally or due to the causal force of some other being. As such, theism is actually a surprisingly simple hypothesis insofar as God is simple (not made up of parts) and intentional or purposive. That God exists *necessarily* is not in itself an arbitrary designation. Existing necessarily or *a se* is part of the very meaning of God. To claim that God is contingent or that God popped into existence one day is akin to claiming that there is a square circle. Intentional explanations are among the most basic kinds that we employ.

Keith Ward rightly points out that Christian theism treats mental causation as basic. He explicitly connects the recognition of consciousness in human beings with the concept of God as an ultimate intentional reality:

> I propose that consciousness, though in the human case it is a factor that emerges from the physical development of the brain, is an irreducible fact, like energy or matter. A conscious state . . . has its own proper reality, and no account of reality that ignores it can be complete.
>
> If that is so, the ultimate constituents of the universe, out of which the whole complex universe is made, cannot just be lumps of matter or fields of force. They must include conscious states. Though animal conscious states—including the human—emerge from complex brains, they are truly emergent, new sorts of reality, and they stand in need of an explanation that cannot be reduced to physical terms alone.
>
> However conscious states come about, once they exist they require not just scientific explanation, but personal explanation. The God hypothesis, at its simplest, is the hypothesis that personal explanation is not reducible to scientific explanation, and that it is prior to scientific explanation. . . . [It] proposes that there is a consciousness that does not depend on any material brain, or on any material thing at all.[15]

For most theists, then, God is a necessarily existing being whose intentional purposive power is foundational to all reality. Timothy O'Connor articulates the theistic claim about God's power:

> A personal necessary being's activity in generating a contingent order is to be thought of, in the first instance, as the direct causing of an internal state(s) of intention that a particular determinate state of affairs obtain. This is not, importantly, to be treated as an elliptical expression for there being some prior state of the agent that brings about, in *mechanistic* fashion, the agent's coming to have the intention. Rather, the intention is irreducibly a product of the agent *qua* agent. This implies as a corollary that the causal power that is manifested in such a case is of a different sort from the mechanistic variety describable by mathematical functions from

circumstances to effects (or from circumstances to ranges of effects, in cases of probabilistic, rather than deterministic, causation).[16]

Let us begin by considering Narveson's line of reasoning. Narveson wants theists to have detailed accounts of how divine purpose or God's will accounts for things. His demands, however, seem to be at odds with our recognition of the concept of basic action. If there are genuine intentional explanations of events, then there must be what some philosophers call *basic action.* These are acts that one does for reasons, but one does them directly and without the mediation of other acts. You might do one thing (say, get your friend's attention) by doing another (calling out to her), but some acts are not mediated. Your calling out to your friend may require a host of factors to come into play in a full explanation (social expectations, language use, personality type, texting). But some acts will be not further accountable by other acts. When you called, you did not do so by willing that certain neurons fire or that your nervous system react in some way; you simply acted.

When Narveson complains that theistic explanation lacks certain mechanisms and causal elements, his complaint cuts against intentional explanations in ordinary human (and other animal) activities. In everyday, bona fide explanations of human agency, there are basic acts that are not further reducible into "impressive detail." (It should also be noted that if there must always be an answer to "how things work" in physical causation, then there can be *no basic physical causes.* This seems counter to many views of causation in the physical world and threatens an infinite regress, as mentioned earlier.) If divine intentions are basic, then so are some human intentions even though the latter are exercised by beings with animal bodies. This implies that Narveson is not successful in ruling out the possibility of theistic accounts. Let me linger on this point.

Imagine that Narveson takes Dennett's strategy and insists that any mental explanations ultimately have to give way to explanations that involve only clearly nonmental causes. This would, however, have the impact of undermining our reasoning. As pointed out in chapter 2, if reasoning takes place, then the embracing of conclusions takes place by virtue of grasping certain reasons. But in nonmental causation there is no reasoning because there are no beliefs, no understanding, no intentions. The difficulty of collapsing or reducing mental, intentional explanations is stated clearly by John Searle:

> So far no attempt at naturalizing content [meaningful beliefs and reasons] has produced an explanation (analysis, reduction) of intentional content that is even remotely plausible. A symptom that something is radically wrong with the project is that intentional notions are inherently normative. They set standards of truth, rationality, consistency etc., and there is no way that these standards can be intrinsic to a system consisting entirely of *brute, blind, nonintentional causal relations.* . . . Indeed, Darwin's major contribution was precisely to remove purpose, and teleology from evolution, and substitute for it purely natural forms of selection.[17]

It will not do to dismiss Searle's point by appealing to the way that computers calculate because they simply are behaving in accord with programs designed by humans. It is unreasonable to believe that computers actually reason or have any beliefs at all. Computers are pure syntactic mechanisms with no intrinsic intentionality.

One more modest point may be added in a reply to Narveson. Scriptural reference to God creating through speech ("God said, 'Let there be light'") may be seen as representing creation as a supremely intentional, purposive act. Among the ancients and many modern thinkers, language usage is considered the high-water mark of intelligence.[18] By describing God as creating through speech, the key thesis is that creation occurs through purposive agency and goodness ("And God saw that it was good") rather than through some thesis about the causal power of divine auditions.

Nielsen's objection to theism seems as plausible as old-style forms of behaviorism in the theory of human nature or the radical materialism explored in chapter 1. Stern forms of behaviorism, such as B. F. Skinner's and radical materialism, deny that there are any first-person experiences or consciousness behind a person writing $E=MC^2$, let alone "PROCRASTINATION DRINKS MELANCHOLY." But once you allow that in human experience there is more than bodily movement and physical processes, why not then be open to there being more to the universe than the spatiotemporal objects and events revealed by science? There is no logical or grammatical error involved in referring to what is "transcendent to the universe" unless you beg the question and define "universe" as all that can be meaningfully thought about or referred to. That, I suggest, is Hepburn's difficulty.

When theists claim that the cosmos is created by God, they do not thereby affirm that *nothing in the cosmos is a reflection of God* or shares in some measure of God's being (for Jews and Christians, humankind is, after all, made in the image of God). Moreover, theists, like most naturalists, see the cosmos as contingent; the cosmos does not necessarily exist, that is, exist as a matter of necessity, as in: it would have been impossible for there not to be a cosmos. While the cosmos is contingent, God exists necessarily. There is no logical blunder in thinking that there is a necessary being who sustains the cosmos; it may be false but not incoherent.[19]

As for O'Shaughnessy's position about scientific versus theistic explanations, he seems to suggest that theism only works in vague contexts. Perhaps O'Shaughnessy thinks that God would only create the wavelength of a spectrum line to only four rather than eight or more decimal places. Obviously, there is no such implied limitation in theism, which recognizes a God of limitless knowledge and power.

Moore's position invites considering the fact that the Cambridge Platonists (and other Christian philosophers from the second century onward) appeal to a host of reasons for believing that there is a God. These reasons range from arguments about why there is a cosmos at all and why it continues in existence, to arguments about the apparent goodness and purposive nature of the cosmos. The emergence of consciousness, moral experience, the apparent experience of God, and more have all been employed in building up powerful theistic arguments. I have addressed and defended many of these arguments elsewhere.[20] The function of this book, however, is not to rehearse these arguments. Here, my aim is to clear the way for experiencing the world as consisting of multiple clues to God and then to explore the nature of such experience in light of Christian reflections on the eternity of God. While it might be beneficial to work up some of my favorite theistic arguments here, I propose to only defend one, central to this book's project, namely, a theistic argument from religious experience. (This is, after all, to be a short book). I shall do so in the next chapter, but first let me make three observations about Moore's specific claim about theism as a hypothesis, and then go on to consider the naturalist concern about the uniqueness of the universe as well as simple, comprehensive explanations.

Moore's comparison of theism to the thesis that "there is a green, three-legged, ten-foot-tall woman in the middle of the road, only you can't detect her" is problematic for at least three reasons. First, theists are not postulating the invisibility of a material being. The invisibility of an incorporeal or nonphysical being is different from the supposed invisibility of a material being. Second, while the God of theism is incorporeal or nonphysical, this is not the same as claiming that God cannot be experienced and thus not "detected." And third, Moore's analogy is hard not to view as hostile because it likens theism to what seems like a freakish finite event with no implications about values. Any serious critique should take seriously the fact that theism (especially in the Platonic Christian tradition of this book) holds that there is a God of awesome, loving power who creates and upholds the whole cosmos. In classical Christianity it is believed that God became incarnate in the Son, who taught us to serve others, as in the Good Samaritan parable; but this model was about serving an actual, visible man who is assaulted by the roadside, not about the imaginary woman in Moore's analogy.

Unique Positions and an Explanation

The choice between theism and naturalism is not, I propose, a matter of one line of reasoning or a single argument, but a matter of a whole network of reasons. In this sense, philosophical reasons may function the way meaning in language functions: there is an interwoven linkage or system of connections. As I.A. Richards puts it, "As the movement of my hand uses nearly the whole skeletal system of the muscles and is supported by them, so a phrase may take its powers from an immense system of supporting uses of other words in other contexts."[21] A similar point can be made in philosophy. Consider, for example, the very existence of consciousness. If you assume at the outset a naturalistic, nonteleological view of the cosmos, then appealing to God's generative, creative power in explaining consciousness or the cosmos will seem like a miracle or a parlor trick. But if you recognize the irreducibility and intelligibility of intentional explanations, matters differ. Theism offers a comprehensive account as to why there is a contingent cosmos at all; and it exists and continues to exist because it is good. Obviously, this claim needs to be assessed in light of the problem of evil (see chapters 5 and 6). Some naturalists think that the cosmos is abhorrent and even claim that if they were the Creator, they would not have created our cosmos.[22] In any case, if you do assume an all-good, purposive, powerful divine Creator, you do have an account of why there is a cosmos at all or why there is gravity and the basic physical laws that allow for life and its evolution.

Naturalists such as J. L. Mackie argue that there are abundant reasoned, scientific explanations of events *within* the cosmos, but they charge that we should not then be led to look for an explanation *of* the cosmos. Mackie writes that we have no guarantee that our reason can operate reliably when it comes to the cosmos as a whole.[23] Perhaps there is no label attached to our cognitive faculties with a warranty, but doesn't it seem like a natural extension of reason to ask about the cosmos itself? Why *does* it exist and persist? I suggest that it seems ad hoc to avoid or rule out such bigger questions, especially as we can consider what appears to be a coherent answer.

What about Dawkins's argument about complexity and simplicity? As suggested earlier, theism can be seen as a profoundly simple hypothesis: God is a singular, purposive, good reality whose comprehensive intention that there be a cosmos at all does not compete with the empirical and theoretic sciences but provides an account as to why science is successful at all. Why should there be a cosmos of physical constraints? The very existence of a Big Bang 13.5 billion years ago with its hydrogen explosion producing helium, the nuclear reactions that eventually produced stars and carbon and eventually planets and life (at least on our planet), is itself an object of awesome wonder inviting us to ask why it is so and why it should endure. The four key elements of our cosmos need to be sufficiently in balance in order for life to emerge and evolve: gravity, the weak force, electromagnetism, and the strong nuclear force binding neutrons and protons in an atom. There would be no chemistry if the electromagnetic force did not exist. If the balance between electromagnetism and gravity were different, then the stars would either be too short-lived (blue giants) or too feeble (red dwarfs) to support life. Naturalism gives us only the thesis that the cosmos is a brute fact, not further explainable as a whole. But we are still left with the question of why there is a contingent cosmos as a whole.

The contrary point that theists are also stuck with a brute fact (what or who made God?) rests on a failure to understand the idea of God in classical theism. If there is a God, then God's essence (what God is) is existence (that God is). God's existence is itself necessary and not contingent. God's very essence or identity is existence.[24] O'Connor offers this exposition of God's necessity:

> The claim that there is a necessary being is the claim that there is a being whose nature entails existence, so that *any* possible world would involve the existence of such an entity. Such a being, we might say, is absolutely invulnerable to nonexistence. By way of relevant contrast, were there a being which was causally immune from destruction (no existing thing or collection of things have the capacity indirectly or directly to destroy it), but whose existence was contingent, it would still, in the end, just *happen* to exist. Were such a being conscious, it could sensibly feel *fortunate* that it exists, even though it owes its existence to no existing thing.[25]

In classical theism, the very concept of God is the concept of a being of unsurpassable, underived excellence; a *contingent* being of great power and knowledge would lack a key divine attribute. In his work on the Trinity, Augustine offers the following brief contrast between the contingency of humanity in contrast to the essential necessity of God: "With the human soul, to be is not the same as to be strong, or prudent, or righteous, or temperate; for the soul is able to exist while having none of these virtues. With God, however, to be is to be strong, to be righteous, to be wise, and to be whatever else you can say of that simple multiplicity or multiple simplicity by which His substance is signified."[26] If

God exists, God's very nature is the nature of superabundant and thus necessary excellence.

What about the uniqueness of the cosmos? Does that forestall inquiry? It has not in terms of physics and cosmology, which have generated competing theories of the natural causes of the cosmos. The uniqueness of the cosmos seems to be no barrier to scientific theorizing. Also, we do have reasonable positions about realities that are unique. Consider, for example, the question of nonhuman consciousness or mental life. We will never become nonhuman animals (unless reincarnation across species is in the offing), and so none of us will know directly what it is like to be a nonhuman animal. The nonhuman animal mind is not unique in the sense that there is only one mind, but the realm of nonhuman consciousness is unique in the sense that we have no direct access to it, so as to compare and assess animal mentality. And yet few of us are content with ruling out the question of whether some nonhuman animals are conscious. (I myself believe that some nonhuman animals are person-like, such as dolphins and the great apes.) The uniqueness of the cosmos and the uniqueness of animal minds do not block inquiry into theism or into a consideration of the case for animal consciousness. Indeed, I suggest that theism offers a profoundly simple, coherent, unified understanding of the cosmos.

Evans on Cranes and Skyhooks

When thinking about big pictures of the cosmos, it is imperative to consider the imagery or metaphors that are employed. Jil Evans has undertaken a trenchant investigation into the way that Dennett and Dawkins use the metaphors of a skyhook versus a crane to describe the difference between a theistic worldview and the philosophy of naturalism. Here is Dennett's set-up of these images:

> Let us imagine that *a skyhook is a "mind first" force or power or process, an exception to the principle that all design and apparent design is ultimately the result of mindless, motiveless mechanicity.* A *crane,* in contrast, is a subprocess

or special feature of a design process that can be demonstrated to permit the local speeding up of the basic, slow process of natural selection, and that can be demonstrated to be itself the predictable (or retrospectively explicable) product of the basic process [emphasis mine].[27]

Dawkins offers a similar portrait of naturalism versus theism.

One of the greatest challenges to the human intellect . . . has been to explain how the complex, improbable appearance of design in the universe arises. The natural temptation is to attribute the appearance of design to actual design itself. . . . The temptation is a false one, because the designer hypothesis immediately raises the larger problem of who designed the designer. The whole problem we started out with was the problem of explaining statistical improbability. It is obviously no solution to postulate something even more improbable. We need a "crane," not a "skyhook." For only a crane can do the business of working up gradually and plausibly from simplicity to otherwise improbable complexity. The most ingenious and powerful crane so far discovered is Darwinian evolution by natural selection. Darwin and his successors have shown how living creatures, with their spectacular statistical improbability and appearance of design, have evolved by slow, gradual degrees from simple beginnings.[28]

Evans rightly points out that these images are anything but fair. "The skyhook isn't just weightless or inadequate; it is an absurdity."[29] Apart from being an evident absurdity, the image of the skyhook belies the claim that theism offers a deep, comprehensive account of the cosmos.

Equating theism with a skyhook ignores the central claim of theism: the very potential for existence in theism is not in a thing, but in a being. The grounding of the cosmos (with all its cranes, suns, cosmic growth and decay, equilibrium and dynamism) in a deeply personal Reality is in a great, omnipresent, intentional being who is anything but (in Dennett's terms) mindless or motiveless. In theism, God is understood as necessarily existing; God is not dependent upon any external causal laws or forces to sustain God in being. Both Dennett and Dawkins write as though if there is a God, God's existence needs to be explained through physical laws. If one imagines God as one of a species, a material thing or a blind force, their view makes sense, but as many have pointed out, . . . Dennett and Dawkins seem to completely misunderstand the nature of theism. . . . If God exists, God's existence is not due to any sort of explanation, or at least not one involving probabilities.[30]

As Evans points out, the image of the crane is designed to assure us that naturalism is well grounded and concrete with its bottom-up explanation, but it also invites the questions: Where is the crane? Why does it exist? Presumably you would have no crane without a cosmos, stable laws of nature, and so on. Why is there such a cosmos rather than not? Although the imagery is designed to silence or to quiet such questions, all such questions are very much alive.

Daniel Dennett, Julian of Norwich, and Comprehensive Accounts

Inquiry into a comprehensive philosophy of life, whether it be an investigation of theism, naturalism, or any number of other big pictures, is rarely cut off from an inquiry into values, and so it is fitting to end this chapter with a contrast between naturalistic and theistic values. This last section is devoted to what some of my students sum up in a succinct, two-word question: So what? The naturalist Dennett's profession of values is a good place to start:

My sacred values are obvious and quite ecumenical: democracy, justice, life, love, and truth (in alphabetical order).

I too, want the world to be a better place. This is my reason for wanting people to understand and accept evolutionary theory: I believe that their salvation may depend on it! How so? By opening their eyes to the dangers of pandemics, degradation of the environment, and the loss of biodiversity, and by informing them about some of the foibles of human nature. So isn't my belief that belief in evolution is the path to salvation a religion? No; there is a major difference. We who love evolution do not honor those whose love of evolution prevents them from thinking clearly and rationally about it! On the contrary, we are particularly critical of those whose misunderstandings and romantic misstatements of these great ideas mislead themselves and others. In our view, there is no safe haven for mystery or incomprehensibility. Yes, there is humility, and awe, and sheer delight, at the glory of the evolutionary landscape, but it is not accompanied by, or in the service of, a willing (let alone thrilling) abandonment of reason. So I feel a moral imperative to spread the word of evolution, but evolution is not my religion.[31]

His invocation of evolution certainly sounds religious: it involves a call for salvation, for spreading "the word;" it involves humility, awe, delight, and glory. It is a pity that Dennett seems to assume that he would be accepting evolutionary theory as a religion only if he abandoned reason or sought a haven in mystery and incomprehensibility. (Defining "religion" so that it is essentially irrational begs the question and is monumentally unfair.)[32] In any case, clearly Dennett invokes many values that theists readily embrace and treat as eternal. In brief, if you value democracy, justice, life, love, and truth, you might be lead to critically investigate Dennett's naturalism.

There are some serious problems with whether evolutionary theory can ground or provide a sufficient basis for Dennett's values. After all, Darwin himself thought that certain events that we presumably find horrifying, such as those causing racial extinction, are natural periods of evolution.[33] Arguably, this would be an instance when the course of evolution conflicts with our sense of Dennett's "democracy, justice, life, love, and truth." But here I suggest a different point: the values identified by Dennett would be magnified in Christian theism. If you are drawn to his values, then you may be drawn not only to consider his naturalism but also to consider a broader, theistic framework.

Consider *The Revelations of Divine Love* by the English mystic Julian of Norwich. In one of her great mystic visions of creation, she observes:

And in this vision he showed me a little thing, the size of a hazel-nut, lying in the palm of my hand, and to my mind's eye it was as round as any ball.

I looked at it and thought 'What can this be?' And the answer came to me, 'It is all that is made.' I wondered how it could last, for it was so small I thought it might suddenly disappear. And the answer in my mind was, 'It lasts and will last forever because God loves it; and in the same way everything exists through the love of God.' In this little thing I saw three attributes: the first is that God made it, the second is that he loves it, the third is that God cares for it. But what does that mean to me? Truly, the maker, the lover, the creator; for until I become one substance with him, I can never have love, rest or true bliss; that is to say, until I am so bound to him that there may be no created thing between my God and me.[34]

In this cosmic setting, Dennett's values would be magnified or intensified. For Julian, it is God's loving creativity that sustains a world in which there is love. The Platonic theistic tradition affirms as eternal values the kinds of values that Dennett identifies. Loving and acting on and for the good is an eternal or everlasting value, not contingent upon whether such love is inconvenient or transient. Dennett's values of democracy, justice, life, love, and truth may receive a magnified, even eternal standing, given theism. While it may seem absurd to link Dennett with Julian of Norwich, some theologians, such as Jacques Maritain, might see Dennett as really seeking God, notwithstanding his claim to atheism. Maritain writes:

> To every soul, even to one ignorant of the name of God, even one reared in atheism, grace proposes, at the moment when this soul deliberates about itself and chooses its ultimate—grace, by the medium of the moral good, proposes as supreme reality to be loved above everything, even if this soul represents this reality to itself under a name which is not its true name— but then (and this is the whole question, and only God knows whether it is so) in thinking under this name *something other* than what it signifies, in going beyond this idol's name—grace proposes the subsistent Good which merits all love and through which and in which our life is saved.
>
> And if this grace is not refused, the soul in question, in opting for this reality, believes obscurely in the true God and chooses really the true God, even though, being in good faith in error and adhering not by its fault, but by that of the education it has received, to an atheistic philosophical

system, it masks this faith-unconscious-of-itself in the true God under formulas which contradict it. An atheist of good faith—a pseudo-atheist, in reality—will in that case have, against his own apparent choice, really chosen God as end of his life.[35]

If Maritain is right, then perhaps Dennett is not completely at odds with Julian. Of course, the case for theism cannot rest on wish fulfillment. The evidence may require us to conclude that Julian's vision is not accessible or justified. Perhaps, like the end of Hemingway's *The Sun Also Rises,* we should resign ourselves and conclude that some relations and goods are not to be. In the novel, Jake Barnes (an American veteran of World War I, a journalist, and the narrator) is in a taxi with Lady Brett Ashley (a fickle, confused, but passionate British socialite whom Jack loves) en route for Brett to renew a relationship with another man. The last lines of the novel are:

> "Oh, Jake," Brett said, "we could have had such a damned good time together." Ahead was a mounted policeman in khaki directing traffic. He raised his baton. The car slowed suddenly, pressing Brett against me.
>   "Yes," I said. "Isn't it pretty to think so?"[36]

The lament is haunting, allowing for a mere hint at what might have been.

In the next chapter let us consider religious experience itself, and its prospect for providing us with a clue or golden cord to the God of Julian of Norwich.

CHAPTER 4

SOME REAL APPEARANCES

No unity with God is possible except by an
exceedingly great love.
—Saint Dimitri of Rostov

In 2011, I attended a philosophy conference in Hong Kong. Near the end
of three days of meetings, we—a group of Chinese and American philosophers—were dining at a restaurant overlooking the port. It turned
out to be a very non–Virginia Woolf dinner party and much more like
that summer night in the 1930s with W. H. Auden. Most of us happened
to be Christians, though we differed considerably on this or that philosophical position. The meal proceeded with personal, at times intimate,
conversations about life's difficulties. Earlier, on the balcony, I was talking to two British philosophers, both Roman Catholic, and one with
considerable experience in monastic life. As the meal ended, however, I
felt dizzy with a sharp pain in my chest. One of my companions asked
calmly, "Are you alright? Would you like some air? Perhaps you should
return to the balcony." I did. And waited. The pain subsided and I was

prepared to rejoin the others. "Wait. Stay as long as you like." The feeling I had then was not exactly akin to Augustine and his mother Monica, but it was close.

Here is the vision of God recorded by Augustine in his *Confessions*. In my case, I was not with my mother and my experience of the divine was not a joint venture through conversation. It was, instead, a more quiet, tangible event. But, consider Augustine:

> Not long before the day on which [Monica] was to leave this life—you knew which day it was to be, O Lord, though we did not—my mother and I were alone, leaning from a window which overlooked the garden in the courtyard of the house where we were staying at Ostia. We were waiting there after our long and tiring journey, away from the crowd, to refresh ourselves before our sea-voyage. I believe that what I am going to tell happened through the secret working of your providence. For we were talking alone together and our conversation was serene and joyful. *We had forgotten what we had left behind and were intent on what lay before us* . . . we laid the lips of our hearts to the heavenly stream that flows from your fountain, *the source of all life* which is *in you*, so that as far as it was in our power to do so we might be sprinkled with its waters and in some sense reach an understanding of this great mystery.
>
> As the flame of love burned stronger in us and raised us higher to-wards the eternal God, our thoughts ranged over the whole compass of material things in their various degrees, up to the heavens themselves, from which the sun and the moon and the stars shine down upon the earth. Higher still we climbed, thinking and speaking all the while in won-der at all that you have made. . . . Then with a sigh, leaving *our spiritual harvest* bound to it, we returned to the sound of our own speech, in which each word has a beginning and an ending—far, far different from your Word, our Lord, who abides in himself for ever, yet never grows old and gives new life to all things.[1]

While I did not exactly pass through "all the levels of bodily objects," still, I did have what seemed like a blissful experience of the sacred, a transport-ing sense of the divine.

Upon reflection, I believe that my experience was informed by a link between my acquaintance saying, "Wait. Stay as long as you like," and one of my favorite lines from Goethe, "Stay, moment, stay, for you are so fair." The line comes from *Faust* and, when first introduced, is a bit sinister. In his pact with the devil (Mephistopheles), when Faust utters this phrase, the devil may take his soul captive. Nonetheless, when Faust finally does say, "Stay, moment, stay, for you are so fair," he has finally come to a different place spiritually. He has seen the futility and disastrous consequences of his lust and sees value in what is at hand. It was the saving character of this delight in the moment that leads God to save Faust, in the end, and frustrate the devil's plan.[2] Whether or not this reading of *Faust* holds up in terms of nineteenth-century German literary criticism, the desire for a moment to stay, to endure outside of clock time, has often colored my deepest experiences in life: falling in love, being with friends recently at Jil's birthday party, conversing with a friend, reconciling with someone after a long period of estrangement, celebrating a friend's recovery from a brain operation, and recalling the sheer joy I knew as a boy at my family's kitchen table. These are moments—moments of depth and grace—when I do not wish to be anywhere else. On the balcony in Hong Kong I felt a similar, almost timeless sense of an arresting, divine presence.

Can these sorts of experiences be taken seriously? A few months after the experience I emailed my fellow philosopher and reported my quasi-Augustinian experience that evening. At the time, I did not tell her about my little encounter with "the fountain of life" but said that I had told my spiritual director about it. My friend replied: "I think you'd better share it with your doctor!" Are these examples of spiritual awareness cases for medicine rather than for metaphysics? Let me offer three cases similar to mine, ranging from the famous to the not so famous. First, William Wordsworth's celebrated poem "Tintern Abbey":

> And I have felt
> A presence that disturbs me with the joy
> Of elevated thoughts; a sense sublime
> Of something far more deeply interfused,
> Whose dwelling is the light of setting suns,

And the round ocean and the living air,
And the blue sky, and in the mind of man:
A motion and a spirit, that impels
All thinking things, all objects of all thought,
        And rolls through all things.[3]

Second, Richard Bucke, a well-known Canadian psychologist of the late nineteenth century, reports:

> All at once, without warning of any kind, he found himself wrapped around as it were by a flame-colored cloud. For an instant he thought of fire, some sudden conflagration in the great city; the next, he knew that the light was within himself. Directly afterward came upon him a sense of exultation, of immense joyousness accompanied or immediately followed by an intellectual illumination quite impossible to describe. Into his brain streamed one momentary lightning-flash of the Brahmic Splendor which has ever since lightened his life; upon his heart fell one drop of Brahmic Bliss, leaving thenceforward for always an aftertaste of heaven. Among other things he did not come to believe, he saw and knew that the Cosmos is not dead matter but a living Presence, that the soul of man is immortal, that the universe is so built and ordered that without any peradventure all things work together for the good of each and all, that the foundation principle of the world is what we call love and that the happiness of everyone is in the long run absolutely certain.[4]

And third, the English Christian theologian Leslie Weatherhead writes:

> For a few seconds only, I suppose the whole [train] compartment was filled with light. This is the only way I know in which to describe the moment, for there was nothing to *see* at all. I felt caught up in some tremendous sense of being within a loving, triumphant and shining purpose. I never felt more humble. I never felt more exalted. A most curious, but overwhelming sense possessed me and filled me with ecstasy. I felt that all was well for mankind—how poor the words seem! The 'well' is so poverty stricken. All men were shining and glorious beings who in the end would

enter incredible joy. Beauty, music, joy, love immeasurable and a glory unspeakable, all this they would inherit. . . . In a few moments the glory departed—all but one curious, lingering feeling. I loved everybody in that compartment. It sounds silly now, and indeed I blush to write it, but at that moment I think I would have died for any one of the people in that compartment.[5]

All three testify to a felt, living presence. For Wordsworth, this presence is felt as animating and intertwined with the natural world. Writing about his experience in the second person, Bucke speaks of a "Brahmic Splendor" that enables him to see himself and the cosmos in terms of love and goodness. Weatherhead's sense of love for others is akin to Auden's mystical experience, cited in the introduction. These cases seem to support the thesis of one of the great twentieth-century studies of religious experience, *The Idea of the Holy*, by Rudolf Otto, who coined the words *numen* and *numenous* to refer to the divine or sacred that is regarded as fascinating (*fascinans*) and mysterious (*mysterium*). If Otto is right, then the experience of the divine is forceful and positive—it is a felt encounter with what appears to be real—as opposed to an inference. Friedrich Schliermacher had earlier analyzed religious experiences in terms of a felt dependency on some greater reality that one infers or interprets as divine. Otto's study led him to think of religious experience in terms of more directly apprehending or encountering what Schliermacher saw as an inference to that on which we (and the cosmos) depend.

There are a range of philosophers today who believe that, in the absence of strong reasons for doubting these visions, we should trust these experiences as evidencing a divine reality. The principle at work here has been called the *principle of credulity* or the *principle of charity*, sometimes articulated as the dictum that we should trust appearances unless we have positive reasons for doubting them.[6] Another way to positively approach religious experiences would be to presume that they are innocent (reliable) until proven guilty (unreliable). Following Kai-Man Kwan, I suggest using the term *critical trust*, such that if a person seems to experience a reality, and the person has some reason to think that the object of experience exists or at least its existence is possible, then the person has reason to trust such an experience as reliable.[7] The trust is *critical* insofar as it is not a principle of gullibility on which *anything goes*. Also, the experience here is understood to be *observational*; an ostensible and apparent experience of X involves X appearing to be present or X being revealed or disclosed as real. On this view, the appearance of X is not the experience of a judgment that some state of affairs is true. There is a difference between a person reporting that it appears to her that God exists (as the result of an argument, for example) versus reporting that God appears to her. Perhaps one helpful way to mark the evidential difference would be to compare two persons who are reading the Bible, a secular naturalist and a "believer" who experiences scripture as an authentic revelation or disclosure of the divine. In the first case, the reader may experience the God of the Bible in the way one experiences a character in a novel (readers may love Gandalf as he appears in *The Lord of the Rings* trilogy), but in the case of the believer, she may have what she believes to be an authentic encounter with (or disclosure of) God or the things of God (awareness of the mercy of God, for example) *through* the Bible.

Before digging into critical objections to trusting ostensible religious disclosures of the divine, I suggest a point that is similar to a theme in chapter 1: we should only reluctantly adopt a method of inquiry that assumes from the outset that a divine disclosure or encounter is unnatural, a violation or contortion of nature or a violation of the very nature of religion. The next section aims to remove some of these obstacles. (In the first chapter I proposed that we should not begin with a methodology like Dennett's, which, from the start, treats as suspect any appeal to the mental.)

Revelation and the Obstacle Course

From time to time, obstacles to accepting revelation claims have been set up. Let us very briefly consider two of these—the philosophical worries about oracles and also about what was known as "enthusiasm"—and then spend a little more time on David Hume and two contemporary thinkers who define "revelation," "experience," "God," and "history" in ways that make the experiential encounter with God unnatural, absurd, antireligious, or a conceptual monstrosity.

Philosophers and Oracles: One reason why philosophy may have flourished in ancient Greece is because philosophical questions were not addressed by oracles or other officially recognized means of divine revelation. If oracles had endorsed philosophical views (for instance, if Apollo, according to the oracle, declared that justice is not as important as beauty), then philosophers who questioned such divinely revealed precepts might have been in even greater danger of accusations of impiety than they were. We have no reason to think that the Oracle of Delphi was ever asked a philosophical question. Philosophers like arguments. This became apparent to me when one of my professors complained, referring to a rival at Harvard University, that he was good on pronouncements but short on arguments: "He thinks he's the bloody oracle of Delphi!"

Ancient philosophers took at least one pronouncement of the Oracle of Delphi seriously. A friend of Socrates was told by the oracle that Socrates was the wisest person in Athens. This pronouncement seems to be what motivated Socrates to challenge others about the nature of wisdom. And Jewish, Christian, and Muslim philosophers have worked fruitfully through the medieval era until today, balancing revelation claims with independent philosophical reflection that did not draw on revelation. Ignoring reports of divine revelation would be like practicing a philosophical inquiry into consciousness, without asking other persons about their thoughts, feelings, and so on.

The danger of enthusiasm: In the seventeenth century the term "enthusiasm" was used to refer to states of mind in which persons may be especially prey to unwarranted beliefs. The worry, expressed perhaps with greatest urgency by Hume and Immanuel Kant, was that courting revelation claims would lead to waves of irrational beliefs.

In reply to this concern, I suggest there is no place that is safe from what used to be called enthusiasm. I know followers of Hume and Kant today who seem entirely subject to waves of irrationality.

Hume's thesis that revelation is unnatural: Hume famously argued that miracles are violations of the laws of nature. There was something unnatural or invasive about reported events in which God is revealed. Hume's case against the rationality of belief in miracles has been widely discussed.[8] Less widely appreciated is the fact that the same strategy that Hume employed against signs of divine intelligence was also used by him to doubt reports of intelligence among black Africans and other nonwhites.

Here is Hume's famous characterization of miracles and his judgment that they cannot reasonably be thought to occur:

> A miracle is a violation of the laws of nature; and as a firm and unalterable experience has established these laws, the proof against a miracle, from the very nature of the fact, is as entire as any argument from experience can possibly be imagined. . . . And as a uniform experience amounts to a proof, there is here a direct and full proof, from the nature of the fact, against the existence of any miracle; nor can such a proof be destroyed, or the miracle rendered credible, but by an opposite proof, which is superior.[9]

Hume holds that all of our experiences that miracles do not occur (we do not routinely observe persons being resurrected, for instance) count against reports of a resurrection.

> A wise man . . . proportions his belief to the evidence. In such conclusions as are founded on an infallible experience, he expects the event with the last degree of assurance, and regards his past experience as full *proof* of the future existence of that event. In other cases, he proceeds with more caution: He weighs the opposite experiments: He considers which side is supported by the greater number of experiments: to that side he inclines, with doubt and hesitation; and when at last he fixes his judgment, the evidence exceeds not what we properly call *probability*. All probability, then, supposes an opposition of experiments and observations.[10]

Hume, however, like Kant, defined Negros (and other nonwhites) so as to make belief in *their intelligence* just as unreasonable as belief in *divine intelligence*. Let me be very clear here: I am not arguing that Hume's case against miracles should be rejected because he was a racist. Rather, I am pointing out that his strategy of ruling out divine intelligence is interestingly similar to his case against intelligence among certain groups of humans. And this raises an important point about values in our inquiry. In a notorious passage, Hume states:

> I am apt to suspect the Negroes and in general all of the other species of men (for there are four or five different kinds) to be naturally inferior to the whites. There never was a civilized nation of any other complexion than white, nor even any individual eminent either in action or specula-tion. No ingenious manufactures amongst them, no arts, no sciences. . . . Such a uniform and constant difference could not happen, in so many countries and ages, if nature had not made an original distinction betwixt these breeds of men. Not to mention our colonies, there are Negro slaves dispersed all over Europe, of which none ever discovered any symptoms of ingenuity. . . . In Jamaica indeed they talk of one Negro as a man of parts and learning; but 'tis likely he is admired for the very sheer accomplish-ments like a parrot, who speaks a few words plainly.[11]

For Hume, there has been a uniform and constant association of whites and superior intelligence, and of nonwhites and inferior or little intel-ligence. He acknowledges reports of exceptions but dismisses this talk in light of his view of the regular, uniform, exceptionless character of nature. He is so convinced of this uniform association that he offers an explana-tion of the ostensible anomalies. It is more probable that blacks merely simulate intelligence, in the way a bird simulates human language, than that they are as intelligent as European whites; presumably, both apparent exceptions can be accounted for in the same way by the laws of nature as Hume conceives them.

When it came to miracle narratives, Hume was convinced that reck-less imagination and wish fulfillment were at work. Primitive people have a natural love of wonder, surprise, and agreeable emotions. Hume may have thought that reports of black or other nonwhite intelligence was akin to miracle narratives, that is, were motivated by wish fulfillment and the love of wonder, surprise, and agreeable emotions.

As it happens, the man from Jamaica referred to by Hume in the pas-sage above was the eighteenth-century Jamaican Francis Williams, who earned a degree from Cambridge University, headed a school, and was known for his Latin poetry. In Hume's day, roughly ten thousand blacks were living and working in London. An eighteenth-century black American poet, Phillis Wheatley, traveled to London, where she publicly wrote and recited poetry. Hume's judgment, however, was fixed against reports of intelligent nonwhites and reports of miracles. Perhaps his assumptions about the nature of black Africans made him unobservant of their successes, just as an individual who does not believe in miracles will not actively search for them in cathedrals.

It seems to me that matters need to be reversed. If the evidence of intelligence, ingenuity, and skill among all peoples seems to some less than perfect, as it often has in the past and even today, Pascal's wager is at hand to motivate people to be open to such evidence. Pascal in the seventeenth century and William James in the nineteenth stressed the importance of values in inquiry: if we have some reason to think there is value to some belief (such as the belief in God or the belief in the dignity of all people), we should not adopt a form of inquiry that will rule out, from the outset, the attainment of such valuable beliefs. Similarly, unless we have positive reasons for thinking theism is incoherent, we should not characterize the ostensible experience of the divine as unnatural.

The Cambridge Platonists were the exact opposite of Hume on such matters. They believed we should treat as natural and good (albeit with a certain amount of critical reasoning) the ostensible experiences of the divine and that we should also be open to the intelligence and goodness of fellow humans, notwithstanding our superficial differences. Peter Sterry's invocation to openness is typical of those in the movement: "Do you so believe that in every encounter you may meet under the disguise of an enemy, a friend, a brother, who, when his helmet shall be taken off, may disclose a beautiful and well known face, which shall charm all your opposition into love and delight at the sight of it."[12] In *The Problem of Slavery in Western Culture*, David Brian Davis credits Cambridge Platonism as laying the groundwork for rejecting the racism and white supremacy of their day. Davis summarizes the Cambridge Platonist outlook as follows:

> For beneath a superficial diversity of cultures one might find a universal capacity for happiness and contentment, so long as man's natural faculties

had not been perverted by error and artificial desire. We must look to primitive man, said Benjamin Whichcote, if we would seek man's moral sense in its pristine state. Natural law, said Nathaniel Culverwel, is truly recognized and practiced only by men who have escaped the corruptions of civilization. If traditionalists objected that savages were ignorant of the Gospel, the answer was that heathen might carry within them the true spirit of Christ, and hence be better Christians than hypocrites who knew and professed all the articles of faith.[13]

On not defining "experience," "history," and "revelation" so as to make revelation or the disclosure of God in experience impossible, unnatural, or implausible: Samuel Fleishacker and Wesley Wildman both employ categories that seem prejudiced against recognizing experiences of God or divine revelation. According to Fleishacker,

> To call God speaking on Sinai (or as Jesus in the Galilee, or, through the angel Givreel, to Muhammad) an "historical fact" is to say that historical methods of investigation would suffice to establish it. But they would not. The very idea of God is the idea of a being beyond all nature, who can control nature itself. . . . No amount of historical evidence could ever prove that that being appeared at a point within the natural course of things. Indeed, the mere idea that they could prove such a thing is a betrayal of the idea of God, a suggestion that God is just one being in the universe among others. For God's appearance in history to be pinned down by scientific investigation would be for God to be subject to the forces of the universe, rather than to be the source of or governor of those forces. A god who can be studied by science is an idol, rather than God, even if there is just one such god, and to believe that the unique God in or on whom the universe is supposed to rest can be known scientifically is to reduce monotheism to idolatry.[14]

Fleishacker caricatures divine revelation as follows:

> Even if, say an apparently disembodied voice, accompanied by thunder and mysterious trumpet blasts, once uttered remarkable accurate prophecies

and deep nuggets of moral wisdom, that would indicate just that there are powers in the universe beyond those with which we are acquainted. Erich von Däniken's hypothesis, in *Chariots of the Gods*, that all supposed religious revelations are really records of visits to earth by intelligent creatures from outer space is very silly, but as an empirical explanation of Sinai, it is better than the hypothesis that the speaker was God. . . . The notion of a power overturning the usual course of events, whose presence can yet be determined by scientific means, is just a notion of an unusual, surprising power within the universe, a sort of magic or a force hitherto relegated to science fiction. The notion of God speaking, or otherwise intervening in human history, defies our very conception of how nature works, and of what a historical event is. So the hypothesis that God has spoken to us can neither be confirmed nor disconfirmed by the findings of historians, or other scientists.[15]

In his *Science and Religious Anthropology*, Wesley Wildman similarly describes experiential revelation as conceptually impaired. According to Wildman, the experiential encounter with God in theistic tradition is the encounter with "disembodied intentionality." God, angels, and ghosts are "discarnate intentional beings." In rejecting theism, naturalists hold that there are "no disembodied forms of intentionality, no disembodied powers."[16]

I offer five succinct replies. First, the idea that if God is the God of nature, then God cannot be manifested in or experienced in the natural world, seems entirely ungrounded. If God can control nature, wouldn't it rather seem to be a limitation of divine agency if God could not act in the created order?

Second, describing revelation or religious experience in terms of "disembodiment" seems at the very least misleading. "Disembodiment" is the contrary of "embodiment" and suggests something impaired or damaged. One may think of the experience of God as the encounter with something incorporeal but not disembodied. (Recall that for integrative dualists, a person is incorporeal and yet is embodied.)

Third, the idea that if God is experienced, then God would become or could become an idol is, at the least, peculiar. A thing need not be experienced to be an idol (someone might even worship the absence of religion), and many things can be experienced without risk of idolatry (myself, for example). Moreover, on some accounts, God experiences (or is at least cognitively aware of) God's self. Would that mean God might become an idol for God?

Fourth, I know of no reason to think that an experience of X entails that X is merely one thing of possibly many things of the same species.

Finally, the term "history" can be used to refer to that which is studied or confirmed through historical inquiry, but it can also simply mean "the past." Someone can believe that (for example) Jesus rose from the dead and that this is a matter of historical fact, without (a) claiming to prove this or (b) claiming that it can be established through historical inquiry. In addition, (c) we believe many things intelligibly about the past and present (free will, moral realism, and so on) without claiming to prove or know or settle the matter through science or philosophy.

Having cleared away some of the obstacles to recognizing the experience of God, let us consider in further detail three objections: the problem of verification, the unreliability of religious experience, and an objection from religious diversity.

The Problem of Verification

Michael Martin and John Schellenberg hold that we have no independent way of confirming the reliability of religious experiences. There is no way to cross-check them. Arguably, in our ordinary perception of material objects, we can simply check whether our perceptions are accurate or not. We may collectively and publicly confirm or disconfirm our sensory experiences. Many religious experiences, however, seem private.

A reply to this objection is that a very strong version of the demand for cross-checking would also threaten ordinary perception. I suggest that skepticism is a powerful challenge to anyone who recognizes the logical possibility that we can all be mistaken about our perceptions of ourselves and the world.[17] How do you know that you are not in the Matrix rather than doing what you appear to be doing, say, riding the subway while reading this book? Knowledge about other people's states of mind also seems to elude ironclad verification.

Wildman addresses this reply, which has been endorsed by the highly respected philosopher William Alston. Alston's strategy, Wildman argues, is to "panic" his readers into thinking that none of their faculties are infallible and incorrigible (incapable of falsehood and revism) and that they must simply be presumed (rather than known) to be reliable.

> In fact, Alston deliberately attempts to induce an epistemic crisis by arguing that all belief-forming practices—from sense perception to memory and from introspection to inductive and deductive reasoning—are subject to the same inevitably circular form of justification. After getting everyone panicked about circularity, and thus about the justification of all belief-forming cognitive practices, he plays the pragmatist's card, or perhaps it is merely a half-card: he points out that there is nothing wrong with circularity. . . . All belief-forming practices operate by venturing beliefs on the presumption of reliability and subsequently evaluating results.[18]

But Wildman argues that such a move is ineffectual. He resists any temptation toward global skepticism and instead trusts naturalistic accounts of our tendency to error and the success of scientific studies of errors. For example,

> Because of this [the possibility of error], psychologists have gone to great efforts to chart the limits of the accuracy of sense perception, discovering the conditions under which we are likely to misperceive, and tying this in to the types of mistakes that human beings are likely to make in forming beliefs. . . . These data on sense-perceptual and cognitive errors have helped cognitive neuroscientists to track down some of the brain processes underlying sense perception, both when it produces accurate beliefs and when it does not. Evolutionary psychologists working on cognition have tried to identify the kinds of evolutionary pressures that produced the sensory apparatus that misfires in precisely these ways.[19]

All of the tests Wildman cites are tests within an overall framework that is presumed to be reliable and not open to question. But I suggest that radical skepticism cannot be dismissed so easily. A philosopher who entertains the possibilities of radical skepticism is wondering about the whole scientific framework, and, because of this, Wildman's diagnosis of why errors are made begs the question; the radical skeptic questions whether the study of errors is itself reliable.

One other point to appreciate: Not all reported religious experiences of the divine are private. From the standpoint of Christian theism, a well-attended Eucharistic service may be an occasion in which many people, together, sense God's love. My experience in Hong Kong was private in the sense that my friend did not share the Augustinian moment, but Augustine's experience was shared with someone, Monica. There are more objections to consider here, but I know of no reason why entire congregations and communities cannot have a collective sense of God's presence. The sense of God need not be akin to Bucke's "flame-colored cloud" or Weatherhead's light; it might simply take the form of feeling a great love for others in which this emotion is experienced as part of a greater divine love.[20]

Unreliability of Religious Experience

Schellenberg acknowledges that there are extensive, impressive traditions of religious experience and interpretation, but he thinks that reported religious experiences are so varied and conflicted that we should not use a principle of charity and assume that they are innocent until proven guilty. Many "religious experiential belief-forming practices" may be known to be false, and so we should be cautious when deciding how to proceed. According to Schellenberg,

> There are ever so many ways in which a doxastic practice [the practice of forming beliefs] could be socially established and yet also [be] the purveyor of utterly false beliefs. Indeed, plenty of actual patterns of belief . . . could be called upon to make this point. One need only think about

false beliefs concerning the shape of the earth, or the alleged inferiority of women, or claimed conspiracies and plots engineered by Jews or other minority groups. And, of course, religion itself presents an obvious and uncontroversial example since the outputs of religious experiential belief-forming practices conflict, and thus not all such practices can be reliable: in virtue of this fact we *know* that *right now* there are socially established religious practices purveying mostly false beliefs, failing to put anyone in effective touch with reality, regardless of their fruits.[21]

For Schellenberg, we would be wise to trust only our basic faculties, our "common inheritance":

> Because we find ourselves unable to *not* form and revise beliefs on the basis of sense perception, introspection, memory, and rational intuition, a certain basic picture of the world has been generated involving birth and conscious experience and physical objects and relations with other conscious beings and the reality of things past and death and also the appropriateness of valuation (presupposed by the humblest desires, and sanctioned by intuition). This picture appears to be our common inheritance. It becomes the very fabric of a human being, affecting one's sense of identity and of connectedness to others and of value and thus also of the appropriate goals, *including intellectual goals*. What we can see here . . . is that we are not independent, truth-registering machines that care not what the truth is and would question everything if we could, but rather deeply *human* inquirers, whose humanity and the basic picture with which it is intertwined do much to shape the nature of our inquiring impulse. Indeed, that very impulse itself, whatever shape it takes, is deeply conditioned by aspects of our "basic picture"; in particular, it is inextricably interwoven with valuation—how could one desire truth or nobly determine to see the truth, whatever it may be, without thinking it *good* to do so? . . . Indeed, with a proper awareness of the nature of that picture, and proper investigative senstitivities, we can see that if we are to embrace religious belief at all, it should be because investigation suggests that we need to do so in order to *properly extend* or *accurately fill out* the picture.[22]

In reply, I suggest that many apparent conflicts in religious experience are less deep than Schellenberg supposes. The same divine reality may be experienced as personal or impersonal, as oceanic and awesome, or as humble and intimate. Many Christian theologians have been open to the ways in which diverse experiences of the sacred may be seen as complementary. Also, Schellenberg seems to radically overstate the extent to which world religions fundamentally disagree. Take Judaism, Christianity, and Islam. If any one of them is true, then do the other two contain "mostly false beliefs"? This is highly unlikely given their common monotheism and massive shared history. Or take Hinduism and Christianity. If Hinduism is true, then is Christianity "mostly false"? Again, this is doubtful. Many Hindus even recognize Jesus as an avatar of Vishnu, a manifestation of the divine.

The widespread testimony to experiential encounters with the divine gives us some reason to believe that our orientation to a divine reality may be very deep indeed and very difficult to separate ourselves from or postpone responding to until we get our "uncontroversial" picture of the world sorted out. And, fundamentally, why should we think that our "common inheritance" is secular or not intertwined with a religious orientation to the world? For significant numbers of religious practitioners, the world itself is experienced as sacred. Schellenberg references the ways in which entrenched social practices have promoted false beliefs (for example, about the shape of the earth), treated women as inferior to men, and so on. A defender of religious experience need not claim that *all* historically embedded belief-formation practices are justified, though for the record there is reason to believe that, historically, world religions have promoted the equality of both women and men; and while Schellenberg mocks "a medieval flat-earther's experiences," it turns out that very few medievalists or large groups of people at any time have believed that the earth is flat.[23] Theistic world religions have many built-in checks on accepting religious experiences as authentic, so being open to the trustworthiness of ostensible experiences of the divine is not a license to accept an anything-goes policy.[24]

Objection from Religious Diversity

Although I have sought to reply to the charge that religious beliefs and traditions contain mostly falsehood—if one is true, then the others are mostly false—let us consider one more specific argument from Schellenberg. While I believe that there is vast accord among religions, there are some differences. So, for example, while most forms of Buddhism agree with most forms of Christianity that greed is bad, compassion is good, and so on, Buddhists adopt a no-self theory of the self. That is, they hold that there is no substantial, individual self. This thesis has been advanced by an appeal to experience. When you engage in self-examination or introspection, do you see yourself? Arguably, you observe feelings, colors, shapes, and so on, but you do not, or so it is argued, actually observe the self.

In these circumstances, how should we weigh the Buddhist experience with, say, a Christian who believes that she is a substantial, individual self, existing over time? We might be tempted to think that while both cannot be right, both are fully justified in holding their different beliefs. Schellenberg does not think so, however. He devises the following thought experiment, in which the religious beliefs and their justification cancel each other out:

> For who *knows* what I would think if I could have *your* experience? A Christian might be inclined to say to members of other traditions: "you would understand my reticence to give up my belief if you could only see what I see." But a better thought here is this: "What if the Christian (or Hindu or the Buddhist . . .) could see from the inside what *all* religious experiments have seen, perhaps in sequence, with a clear memory afterward of what she had seen—would her belief be affected *then?*" Presumably the answer is "perhaps yes, perhaps no." . . . Certainly one's own experience can provide no grounds for going one way or the other on *this* matter. (That I have a powerful experience apparently of Christ may entail, at least for that moment, that I form a religious belief about Christ, and this belief may entail the falsity of incompatible beliefs from other traditions; but neither of these things entails that, *should I experience the*

*world as does a Hindu or a Buddhist, I would not conclude that their experi-
ence was more illuminating and convincing than mine*) [emphasis mine].[25]

I don't find Schellenberg's case convincing. One way to respond to this
thought experiment is to point out that both Buddhist and Christian
religious experiences can be veridical. I shall develop this point from the
Christian perspective of persons being substantial individuals. We can acknowledge that if you are looking for a self that appears in your visual or
auditory field as an object, then you will not see or hear a self; but if you
allow that the self is the one who is seeing and hearing, then your experience of the self is evident and continuous. With pain, for example, I am
feeling a state of myself, I am experiencing myself as a substantial reality.[26] In this sense, a defender of the substantive view of the self can fully
acknowledge the merits of a Buddhist's experience but without thereby
holding that the Buddhist account covers the self as a whole.

The above point about the observability of the self brings up another
issue. Why aren't reports of sensing God more prevalent? Actually, I believe that they are quite extensive. But one reason why they might be
even more extensive than currently recognized is because of the conceptual frameworks that we employ. I suggested above that one reason why
persons might hold that they do not have a substantial self is because, if
they had or were such a self, then they would observe it as they would
observe an object in a visual field. It may well be that a shift in perspective
widens the area. A parallel case may arise concerning religious experience.
Imagine, for the sake of argument, that Christian theism is true, and let
us further imagine that you attend a Eucharist service. While you are an
agnostic, you have a vague sense (perhaps stimulated by a blend of music,
readings, and such) that there is "a spirit that impels all thinking things,"
along the lines of Wordsworth's "Tintern Abbey." Now, perhaps this sense
is no more than your entertaining a vision of God and your contemplating, "Well, maybe life might be like that." But it might also be (given
the truth of Christian theism) an actual *appearing* or an *encounter*. The
felt difference between an *appearing* and merely contemplating (favor-
ably but not fully affirming) may be seen in comparing two experiences
involving the Bible. In what we might call the *scholarly experience,* you

may encounter the God of the Bible insofar as you entertain (and perhaps critically evaluate) God as a figure or subject in the Bible. This may be akin to studying a figure in any novel. But there is a distinctive difference between that and the experience that one is encountering God as a living reality *through* the Bible. The latter may have an evidential value that the first does not have. In the second experience, one senses the presence of a subject as a living reality and not merely the presence of a subject matter upon which one is reflecting.

As for the case of someone having "a powerful experience apparently of Christ" (as I have had and appear to continue to have), most philosophers today tend to think that such experiences need to be assessed in comprehensive terms. My Hindu friends do not deny my experience, though rather than recognize Christ as the unique incarnation, they see Christ as one of many manifestations of the divine. I suggest that if the Christian "could see from the inside" what a Hindu experiences and vice versa, then there would not be a cancelling out of claims. We would together simply have more to share and compare! As for whether this "inside seeing" brings about a conversion or an attempt to be a Hindu-Christian will depend on more than "inside seeing."

Religious Experiences Explained through Sociology, Anthropology, Neurology, and Psychology

In modern thought, a substantial case has been made for the idea that wish fulfillment, guilt, and social training and formation account for reported religious experiences. The most recent line of reasoning behind this objection is that human beings have an overactive habit of attributing intentionality, purpose, or meaning to events that lack intentions, purposes, or meanings. It is argued that this tendency is responsible for religious experiences triggered by rites, meditation, and so on. Imagine that we have an airtight neurological account that correlates experiences such as Wordworth's, Bucke's, and Wheatherhead's with predictable brain patterns.

This argument seems to cut both ways. If theism is adopted out of wish fulfillment, so then might naturalism or any number of theories. Perhaps social training and formation in nontheistic or aggressively secular cultures explain why some persons in these cultures do not experience the divine. Perhaps the theory that other people believe what they wish is because people wish that it were true. Maybe we can identify all the neurological events that correlate with thinking that there is no God or doing mathematics.[27] If we do have a natural, "in-built" tendency to attribute meaning to events, perhaps this is because there is some meaning or value to being. I suggest that the tendency to experience the divine cannot be swept away by this strategy without threatening our reasoning in many areas that seem vital, such as in ethics. We do seem to have a built-in tendency to avoid suffering and perceive it as bad (at least in our own case), but is this not really evidence that it is bad and only reflects wish fulfillment?[28]

A critic may not be at all content with this rejoinder. Perhaps the accusation of wish fulfillment cuts both ways. Richard Dawkins's charge that religious faith is infantile can be as unhelpful as a theist returning the favor and casting Dawkins himself as infantile.[29] But, it may be argued, if one can successfully give a good reason for thinking that people could have apparent experiences of God, even if God does not exist, then the apparent experiences lose their evidential value. Imagine, for example, that in a room there is a light on that makes all the objects look yellow. Your observation that something is yellow has no evidential value because the objects would appear yellow even if they were, say, white or gray.

Two points need to be appreciated in reply. First, if you do not know that there is a yellow light that makes all objects appear yellow, then you should trust your observation of yellow objects. Similarly, if you don't know that naturalism is true (or theism false), trusting apparent theistic experiences seems perfectly sensible. Second, none of the studies or naturalistic projects of explaining religious experience convinces me that we would have the apparent positive experience of the divine if there is no God. This claim would require a detailed argument that goes beyond the scope of this short book.[30] But a broader point can be stated succinctly,

if classical theism is correct: there would be no experience of God unless God exists, because there would be no cosmos at all if God does
not exist.[31]

Further Steps

Some of the case studies cited in this chapter involve a sense of the divine coming upon the subjects (including me) as a dramatic, unexpected
external force. But there are also ample cases of when the sense of the
divine may be more ordinary and quiet, as I suggested in the example of
someone's simple attendance at a Eucharist service, or in the course of
studying scripture. There is also room for appreciating how one might
develop habits or dispositions to be open to such experiences. As Peter
Donovan writes,

> A religious believer who looks on the world as a domain in which God
> may possibly manifest himself (in one way or another) has the potential
> for a whole range of significant experiences not open to the person with-
> out such a world-view. He does not just *view* the world in a religious way.
> He lives within it, and acts and responds and experiences its events and
> happenings (including his own feelings and states of mind) with the pos-
> sibility in his mind that in doing so he may be coming in touch not just
> with the world and other people in it, but with the activity and manifesta-
> tions of God.[32]

At the risk of employing a rather pedestrian analogy, consider the
topic raised in the last chapter about animal minds. Imagine that you become convinced that some nonhuman animals are conscious, intelligent
beings on the basis of various control experiments involving the use of
tools, mirror self-recognition, anatomy, and behavior. Having come to
that conclusion, you interact with such animals (whether as a professional
field biologist or as someone who, like myself, takes his dog to pet therapy
programs in area hospitals) in a way that will involve a greater receptivity
to animal mental life. A similar, perhaps less Pickwickian point, can be

made about working with or raising prelinguistic human children. Some philosophers have held that nonlanguage users do not, even cannot, have beliefs. I find this monumentally implausible; if one cannot have beliefs prior to language acquisition, then how could one acquire a language? But compare two philosophical parents, one of whom is convinced that prelinguistic children have no beliefs, while the other is open to the possibility. The latter would, I suggest, have a greater ability and opportunity to apprehend a child's interior, mental life. Something similar may be the case in terms of spirituality and religious experience. An openness to a sense of the divine may increase its likelihood.

Norman Kemp Smith concludes an essay defending the intelligibility of experiencing the divine by noting how individual experiences can be bolstered or enlarged through community or involvement in discipline: "Divine Existence is more than merely credible: it is immediately experienced; and is experienced in increasing degree in proportion as the individual, under this or that of its great traditional forms, is enabled to supplement his initial experiences by others of a more definite character. And in Divine Existence, as thus revealed, the non-creatureliness, that is, the otherness of God, is fundamental."[33] Furthermore, many of the religious experiences in theistic tradition are not just golden cords leading one to, say, an awareness of God, but they speak also to what might be called a *communion* between the soul or person and God. R. G. Collingwood emphasizes this outcome, connecting the person with God through prayer:

> A painter makes his picture perfect by looking back from moment to moment at the vision which he is trying to reproduce. A scientist perfects his theory by testing it at every point by the facts of nature. So the religious life must come back again and again to the contemplation of its ideal in God. But God is a person, not a thing; a mind, not an object. We contemplate objects, but we do not contemplate persons. The attitude of one mind to another is not contemplation but communion; and communion with God is prayer. Prayer may not be the whole of religion, but it is the touchstone of it. All religion must come to the test of prayer; for in prayer the soul maps out the course it has taken and the journey it has

yet to make, reviewing the past and the future in the light of the presence of God.[34]

Before moving forward to the ideas of eternity and time, however, we must pause to take on the problem of evil in the course of two chapters. The experience of evil and the possibility or the promise of redemption are key elements in the Christian longing for the divine, and thus the next two chapters are essential for the task of this book as a whole. After all, if we are to take experiences seriously, we need to take into account those that seem quite the opposite of Augustine and Monica's. Consider the following experience that Jean-Paul Sartre records of his narrator in the novel *Nausea*:

> I looked anxiously around me: the present, nothing but the present. Furniture light and solid, rooted in its present, a table, a bed, a closet with a mirror—and me. The true nature of the present revealed itself: it was what exists, and all that was not present did not exist. The past did not exist. Not at all. Not in things, not even in my thoughts. It is true that I had realized a long time ago that mine had escaped me. But until then I believed that it had simply gone out of my range. For me the past was only a pensioning off: it was another way of existing, a state of vacation and inaction; each event, when it had played its part, put itself politely into a box and became an honorary event: we have so much difficulty imaging nothingness. Now I knew: things are entirely what they appear to be—and behind them . . . there is nothing.[35]

Comparing Sartre's and Augustine's visions, like assessing cosmic goods and ills, is akin to judging ordinary perception. In the absence of any knowledge of our solar system, one may perceive the moon to be small. A friend doing some missionary work in Africa in 1969 was unable to convince a tribal gathering that an American astronaut took a twenty-minute walk on the moon; his claim only met with laughter as they explained that it was impossible because the moon was too small. Knowledge of perspective and distance helps us adjust our judgments, and something similar is involved in religious experience. If naturalism is true and theism false, then ostensible experiences of God turn out to be far smaller or less significant than they appear; if theism is true, however, then the ostensible experience of God may turn out to be the faint glimmer of that which is overwhelming in goodness, power, and knowledge. A still further similarity is in play about good and evil. Is the evident appearance of evil so massive that it eclipses the possibility of an all-good God? Is Sartre's vision or Augustine's vision more disclosive of being (or, in Sartre's case) nothing? When Sartre writes that "things are entirely what they appear to be," is he portraying a hard, no-nonsense realism or a truncated view of what may be seen as rich and expansive?

CHAPTER 5

IS GOD MAD, BAD, AND
DANGEROUS TO KNOW?

It is tempting to conclude that if [God] exists, it is
the atheists and agnostics that he loves best, among
those with any pretensions to education. For they
are the ones who have taken him most seriously.

—Galen Strawson

During a philosophy conference at Macalester College, a young man was
presenting a paper on the problem of evil. There was something detached
and aloof about the way he set the problem before us: "Let us assume, for
the sake of argument, that there is a triple-A God." By this, he explained,
he referred to a God that is All-powerful, All-knowing, and All-good.
In any event, he set up the problem of evil as "the problem of the poisoned water." Imagine that a fiend has put poison in a glass of water. An
innocent person comes along, drinks the glass of poisoned water, and
dies. This is a clear case of the fiend doing a wrong act, and he is fully

responsible for it. But now imagine that there is a bystander who saw everything and had the power to intervene but did not. Isn't that person also responsible for the preventable, wrong death? The bystander is like God, or so the young man argued.

Is God a Bystander?

As noted in chapters 3 and 4, the God of Christianity creates and sustains the cosmos; and, if Augustine, the Cambridge Platonists, and Auden are correct, then God may even be encountered experientially. The chief difficulty with setting up the problem of evil along the lines of poisoners and bystanders lies in not sufficiently appreciating that God, in Christianity, is active both as Creator and as a power within the cosmos. So, in taking on board the three As, or Os, we cannot view the question as simply as, say, analyzing a crime scene. If one thinks that God's not preventing an evil event counts as a reason for thinking that there is no God, then one needs to take seriously what may be called the ethics of creation. What do you think are the ethical constraints (if any) that should govern what a good God creates? The question may seem preposterous. Are our ethical judgments and rules the sort of standards that can be used to measure which galaxies would be good to create? Although the questions are wild, if one is going to think and talk about (as well as love) God as good, even supremely good, we will need to rely on our ordinary moral judgments but try to extend them to cover a truly extraordinary, cosmic scale.

In an effort to adapt such a cosmic point of view, I can rephrase the problem of evil along the following lines: Is it compatible with God's goodness for God—as an all-knowing, all-good, all-powerful being—to create and sustain a cosmos that contains profound goods (stable laws of nature), plant and animal life, consciousness, moral experience, and some experiential awareness of God, and yet there is profound suffering and pain brought about by floods and droughts, murder, rape, birth defects, and crippling diseases? There is beauty too, such as in the birth of a child, art works, and romantic love, but there are also miscarriages, cruelty, and mass killing. If there is an all good-God, then all evils are contrary to

God's will and nature; each murder is a case in which something sacred is destroyed (the victim) and perverted (the murderer misuses his power). God has given freedom to human creatures that can be used horrifically or lovingly in valuable relations of interdependence. He acts in the world to prevent some harm through answers to prayers, but not all prayers are answered. His nature and will are revealed to many creatures, and, if Christianity is true, then God has become incarnate as Jesus to redeem creation in this life as well as through an afterlife in union with God.

In asking this question we build into the inquiry a thesis that goes underappreciated in debates about God and evil: historically, the majority of Christian theologians holds that certain events are genuinely evil, are contrary to God's will and nature, and thus should not occur. Such events are not justified or permissible. Some Christians have held a very strong view of divine providence according to which everything that occurs has a purpose. But the vast preponderance of Christian teaching remains clear: murder, rape, soul-destroying illnesses, and other horrors are against God's will and count as profound wrongs and breakdowns contrary to God's intended created order. To fill out this vital point, consider the following distinction.

Redemption Is Not Justification

When one justifies evil, one typically argues that some end or greater good made the evil necessary. In warfare, if repelling an unjust invading force requires the death of innocent, noncombatant civilians, then such deaths may be justified. Or, to take a less controversial case, imagine that the only way to foil and escape from a belligerent assailant is to lie. Here, something that is otherwise wrong becomes permissible, maybe even good. (It sounds odd to ever claim that it is good that there is evil, but on a utilitarian framework—in which the end may justify the means—this occurs).

Redemption is different. Here, it is always the case that what was wrong ought not to have occurred. So, imagine two people, Pat and Kris, in what begins as a good relationship. Eventually, Pat betrays Kris, and Kris considers severing the relationship. Imagine that Pat repents, however, and out of love they reconcile. Imagine further that the couple discovers the great good of reconciliatory love and the extraordinary realization of the good of being loved by another person under the worst of conditions. Isn't this outcome a greater good than the couple would ever have achieved if there had been no betrayal? In a *framework of justification*, one might even conclude that betrayal was good, but in a *framework of redemption* this is not the case. Each party has discovered a great, transforming good, and yet the betrayal remains unchanged as an evil. The distinction between justification and redemption is important to take seriously, lest one forget the truly horrific nature of evil as a profound violation of God's will and nature.

I am not suggesting that issues of justification are wholly out of place in addressing the problem of evil. It only needs to be stressed that if God seeks to redeem persons, then the past evil is still not to be seen as itself good or permissible. On some accounts, mercy, whether shown by God or humans, is in tension with justice. That is, cases may arise when a person both deserves and ought to be punished, but a good ruler or magistrate may show mercy by reducing the punishment. In the context of the problem of evil, one needs to be open to the possibility that while an all-good God ought to punish the wicked person, God's goodness may also be compatible with God's not punishing but, rather, redeeming the wicked.[1]

Love of God

In my epigraph at the beginning of this chapter, I quoted Galen Strawson's comment about atheists and agnostics taking God more seriously than believers. Presumably, Strawson supposes that if there is a God (with three As), then God is guilty of great cruelties in allowing enormous, undeserved suffering. An atheist may be said to love the idea of God insofar as an atheist might wish that God did exist, because then there would be no evil at all or no undeserved suffering but only bliss. In a sense, Strawson may be backed up by an observation by Erasmus: "He who does not believe God exists is less insulting to his fellow man than he who believes

God is cruel or vain."[2] But if we shift the ground a bit, we can develop a different response to Strawson.

Imagine two universes exactly like ours in its present state in every way except one. Both universes have equal amounts of suffering and pleasure, struggle and disappointment, happiness and tragedy. In one universe, however, there is a Creator-God who is lovingly seeking through prophets, an incarnation, and religious experience to call all people to a life of fulfillment, and this God will indeed offer redemption to everyone in this life or the next. In that universe, men and women die; they are poisoned or murdered or die naturally, but they are not thereby annihilated. Through God's omnipotent love, they are called from death to life. Now, compare that with a universe exactly like ours: the same degrees of suffering, death, happiness, and sorrow. But imagine that in such a universe, there is no all-good, all-knowing, all-powerful God who seeks redemption for the Creation. In that universe, death is annihilation. Now, two questions: first, which universe do you think contains more good? And second, if one were truly to play out Strawson's schema, do you think a person who truly loves God or the idea of God would prefer the second universe?

Reflections on the problem of evil are incomplete as long as one neglects the question of why evil is a problem. Clearly, thinkers from ancient Greece onward have wondered why there is suffering and tragedy, and this has been seen as problematic if there is one or more divine realities that may prevent it. But if one denies that there is any divine, good reality, to what extent is evil a problem? For example, the loss of my sister-in-law to cancer is a problem because she was a talented, precious human being who, had she lived, would have continued to flourish and bring joy to others. But if you are, as is Strawson, a determinist, there is a sense in which her death was unpreventable (given the laws of nature, antecedent conditions) and not at all in violation of nature or natural law. Her premature death was fixed from the Big Bang billions of years ago. Similarly, if Strawson is right, all your acts in the future cannot be freely altered by you in a way for which you can take moral responsibility. In this worldview, evil is not a problem insofar as it should not occur given the state of the world, the laws of nature, and so on.

Alternatively, if theism in the Cambridge Platonist tradition is true, then evil is a violation, a preventable sacrilege that, again, should not occur; it is out of union with the will and nature of the all-good Creator. Our apprehension or even perception that evil is a problem can, in some respects, be seen as a golden cord or clue that we are oriented toward some transcendent good. This is not a matter of mere wish fulfillment: if we wish that life were better than it appears, then it is better than it appears. Still, the fact that we do rebel against the state of the world—its suffering and its unmet needs—can be a sign that we are so made as to desire that which not only is truly fulfilling but also is a transcendent good.

Consider now four major objections or sides to the problem of evil: the problem of freedom; the problem of innocent victims; the hiddenness of God objection; and the vices of God objection.

The Problem of Freedom

In an important work, *On What Matters*, Derek Parfit argues that none of us have a morally significant kind of freedom (sometimes called libertarian freedom). In essence, Parfit claims that for us to be genuinely responsible for doing X rather than not-X, we would have to be able to create ourselves. Any decision that we might make, however, stems from our character. Therefore, it is impossible for someone to (as it were) step away from herself and shape her own character, because any decision to shape her character will reflect her character. Those who defend libertarian freedom, in contrast, claim that persons act on the basis of the reasons they choose to adopt, and that this is a genuinely free act (the person could have done otherwise). Parfit argues that such an appeal to reason is unintelligible.

> When someone acts for some reason, however, we can ask why this person acted for this reason. In some cases, the answer is given by some further reason. My reason for telling some lie, for example, may have been to conceal my identity, and my reason for concealing my identity may have been to avoid being accused of some crime. But we shall soon reach the

beginning of any such chain of motivating reasons. My ultimate reasons for telling my lie may have been to avoid being punished for my crime. When we reach someone's ultimate reason for acting in some way, we can ask why this person acted for this reason, rather than acting in some other way for some other reason. If I had a self-interested reason to try to avoid being punished, and a moral reason not to tell this lie, why did one of these reasons weigh more heavily with me, so that I chose to act as I did? This event did not occur for some further motivating reason. So the suggested . . . alternative here [this event was either fully caused or partly random] disappears.[3]

Libertarians who are incompatabilists, such as Peter van Inwagen, Roderick Chisholm, Stewart Goetz, Richard Purtill, Daniel Robinson, John Foster, and (to appeal to a favorite philosopher of mine) C. A. Campbell, claim that persons have a basic—that is, not further explicable—power to act and the power to do otherwise than they act, given all antecedent and contemporary events and the prevailing laws of nature. Campbell concedes that from the outside, from a third-person or external point of view, the case for libertarian agency or even the nature of such agency seem mysterious. It is only from the first-person point of view that "agentive power" (a term that Robinson deploys to describe libertarian power, or the morally significant power of agents) makes sense. According to these libertarian philosophers, the phenomenology of what it is to be an agent discloses or brings to light our ostensible power to act and to do other than what we do.

How do we know that such a positive account of our free action is wrong? In the passage from Parfit cited above, do we have reason to believe that there cannot be a basic agentive power? Imagine that someone decides to lie. Might it be that the reasons for lying were her reasons because she made a decision to act that way when she could have done otherwise? As Campbell notes, the thesis of libertarian agency is that persons do have a basic power, a power that is not determined by some other force. "Such critics [as Parfit] apparently fail to see that if the Libertarian could say why [give a deterministic account of a choice], he would already have given up his thesis."[4]

Parfit, however, claims to have a decisive argument against this stance: "When other writers try to describe some third alternative to some act's being fully caused, or partly random, it is a decisive objection to such claims that they are incomprehensible."[5] Interesting. I can accept that Parfit himself does not comprehend the concept of free agency as defended by Chisholm, van Inwagen, Robinson, and so on, but why does that give me or others reason to believe that Chisholm and company do not know what they are talking about, and that the concept of agentive power is incomprehensible? Parfit, I take it, does not think that the failure of other philosophers to comprehend his notion of reason is a decisive reason against his position. And because he believes that normative reasons are irreducible, Parfit should not rule out in principle the idea that there might be agentive powers, which are not reducible to non-agentive powers.

A thought experiment may be helpful here. Consider the following story of mine, which tries to make freedom—the kind of freedom Parfit finds incomprehensible—an evident, everyday reality.

Maria had just given a talk against the coherence of libertarian agency. She felt good; in fact, she felt very cool as she had composed her paper while working out at a gym and she had lost that weight that was bothering her. Why, she thought to herself, even Arthur had taken notice. Arthur? Why, yes, he was a friend and was married. But hadn't he been a bit flirty when he asked her to come by the hotel room for a drink after her talk? Why not? What could go wrong? Well, she thought, maybe I shouldn't. But her own husband had an affair three years ago, and she had forgiven him. Wouldn't she be forgiven? Maria went to the lobby and called the desk: "Please put me through to Dr. Arthur Taylor." Her heart was racing. Should she say: "Sorry, Arthur, I am exhausted, and need to call it an early night." Or: "Guess who gave the Dewey lecture and got a standing ovation? You're talking to the lady right now! Let's raise a glass, and maybe more. What's your room number?" She still had no idea what to do when Arthur answered: "Disappointing news, darling, the reception for the Dewey lecturer only includes one person. But he is in room 320 and is most excited." "Sorry, Arthur!" she found herself saying, "sorry to be a pill but I have to take an early flight"—which was a lie—and then she thought she better make the lie bigger. "I got a call from Jim and our oldest is sick." She paused: am I going to lie out of self-interest or be honest? Honesty. She could walk away from it and stick to the lie. She decided instead: "Actually, Arthur, to be honest, I think if I came to the room, things would get way out of hand." "What are you talking about?" "I'm pretty pathetic when it comes to self-restraint. Let's meet with Mark and Jilly over breakfast at 9 tomorrow morning instead." "You got it." Maria closed the line. She thought: I made the right decision; if I had gone to see him, there might have been no turning back. Or did she? She might—right now—be having the time of her life. Back in her room, she went to the mini-bar. After a second gin and tonic, she wondered about the feelings she had during the conversation. You know, she said to herself almost out loud, it really felt like things could have gone either way. I could have gone up there, but I decided to resist it. Did I make the right decision? Am I right in my Dewey lecture that libertarian freedom is incoherent? She was asleep soon after that. The breakfast was amusing but quite unsexy. By the time she got back to her office on Monday, Maria was on the phone: "Hannah," she called her good friend Hannah Dexter. "How do I retract my Dewey lecture? Either I need to withdraw it or add a footnote that I now think libertarian agency is coherent and, well, actually, I think at least some of us have it." "What the hell are you talking about?" "Um, let's just say something happened at the convention that made me change my mind." Hannah, sighed: "Crap, Maria, you go to a convention and now you're in bed with libertarianism." "Close, but I did not sleep with libertarianism." Maria smiled when she realized that Arthur was a libertarian, being a former graduate student of Peter van Inwagen.[6]

The story may seem banal to some readers, but it in fact addresses the bewilderment of a highly prominent professor. Although I do not claim to know that libertarian concepts of agency are coherent and plausible, any number of examples from everyday life suggest that it is. As C. A. Campbell puts it, libertarian agency seems unintelligible only if we rule out first-person phenomenology: "Those who find the libertarian doctrine of the self's causality in our decisions inherently unintelligible find it so simply because they restrict themselves, quite arbitrarily, to an inadequate standpoint: a standpoint from which, indeed, a genuinely creative activity, if it existed, never could be apprehended."[7]

Consider an objection: Isn't the above story a tad fatuous? In reply, consider another story: "James was exhausted. Squaring a circle while going backwards in time is tough work. He had earlier violated the principle of the indiscernibility of identicals and finally found a green idea that sleeps furiously." But even highly detailed, gripping stories about squaring a circle, told at the level of detail and emotion of, say, George Eliot's *Middlemarch*, cannot make coherent the claim that you can have an object that both has and lacks four right angles at the same time. In contrast, if there is anything to the libertarian account of free agency, especially along the lines of Campbell, then there will be something it is like to exercise such agency. The libertarian can call on coherent stories as examples, even if his philosophical account of free agency may be false. When a philosopher denies this freedom, a defender has an opportunity to try to bring the experience into focus.

The art of pursuing virtue through grace and freedom has a rich role in Christian theism. There are significant differences among theologians concerning the scope of freedom. Martin Luther, for example, stresses divine grace, whereas the Cambridge Platonists stress freedom *and* divine grace. But those emphasizing human freedom did not use the image of *causa sui* (being self-caused); the closest they came is a very different image, that of birth. Gregory of Nyssa was a firm opponent of slavery and the idea that a person is fully owned by his society, family, or emperor. "We are in some manner our own parents," writes Gregory, "giving birth to ourselves by our own free choice in accordance with whatever we wish to be."[8] Far from involving a logical contradiction, I suggest, we can and do reshape ourselves when we choose between possible futures. We see "the way you are" as not in itself a fixed, settled matter in an instant *t*. In a sense, it would be more accurate to claim that "the way you are" includes many possibilities, many different ways you may come to be.

The fact that we might elect to be different than we are was used by the Cambridge Platonist Peter Sterry to argue for a greater receptivity toward others. He reasoned, "Had my education, my acquaintance, the several circumstances and concurrences been the same to me, as to this person from whom I now most of all dissent, that which is now his sense and state might have been mine."[9] Sterry uses this observation to bolster allegiance to the Second Commandment, loving one's neighbor as oneself: "Have the same just, equal, tender respects and thoughts with the same allowances of another, which you require from him to yourself."[10]

One further point about freedom is worth making. Christian theists have traditionally valorized the concept of a creature's freedom as a key link with the divine: being free is part of what makes us in the image of God. But the stress on freedom is usually accompanied by a stress on the good of interdependence. In her *Dialogue,* Catherine of Siena records this revelation from God:

> I [God] have distributed [all virtues and graces] in such a way that no one has all of them. Thus have I given you reason—necessity in fact—to practice mutual charity. For I could well have supplied each of you with all your needs, both spiritual and material. But I wanted to make you dependent on one another so that each of you would be my minister, dispensing the graces and gifts you have received from me. So whether you will it or not, you cannot escape the exercise of charity! Yet, unless you do it for love of me, it is worth nothing to you in the realm of grace. . . . In loving me you will realize love for your neighbors, and if you love your neighbors you have kept the law.[11]

If Saint Catherine is right, then interdependence alone is not itself good, but it is a great good when informed by gracious love.

The Problem of Innocent Victims

Even if we can defend the claim that we can be free and responsible for our characters, it seems that many persons and nonhuman animals suffer, and not for any fault of their own. The problem of animal suffering is particularly difficult to assess because we do not know its scope. Indeed, in terms of animal life, suffering seems built into the process of evolution.[12] While historically there has been significant debate over whether evolution would be worthy of an all-good God (would an all-good God exercise a series of special creations, much as we find in Genesis 1?), recent ecology seems to understand animal predation in the wild as something good, or at least not something that we should seek to abolish or police. Overall, the idea of the natural world without animal suffering or predation seems problematic. Holmes Rolston III takes up the possibility of a natural world with less suffering:

> Could, should God have created a world with only flora, no fauna? Possibly. Possibly not, since in a world in which things are assembled something has to disassemble them for recycling. In any case, we do not think that a mere floral world would be of more value than a world with fauna also. In a mere floral world, there would be no one to think. . . . Could we have had only plant-eating fauna, only grazers, no predators? Possibly, though probably we never did, since predation preceded photosynthesis. Even grazers are predators of a kind, though what they eat does not suffer. Again, an Earth with only herbivores and no omnivores or carnivores would be impoverished . . . no horns, no fleet-tuned eyesight and hearing, no quick neural capacity, no advanced brains. We humans stand in this tradition, as our ancestors were hunters. . . .
>
> Life preys on life; all advanced life requires food pyramids, eating and being eaten. Humans are degenerate in the sense that we cannot synthesize all that we need, compared with, say, the flora, which are autotrophs. But in such degeneracy lies the possibility of advancement.[13]

If Rolston is right, predation and the evolving of plant and animal life are ecologically interwoven and transformative. An alternative biology without suffering would be unrecognizable to us, perhaps requiring a special creation in which God creates only herbivores fully formed under ideal conditions.

Peter van Inwagen observes that intelligent life is almost unimaginable without extensive natural evolutionary suffering:

> Only in a universe very much like ours could intelligent life, or even sentient life, develop by the nonmiraculous operation of the laws of nature.

And the natural evolution of higher sentient life in a universe like ours essentially involves suffering, or there is every reason to believe it does. The mechanisms underlying biological evolution may be just what most biologists seem to suppose—the production of new genes by random mutation and the culling of gene pools by environmental selection pressure—or they may be more subtle. But no one, I believe would take seriously the idea that conscious animals, animals conscious as a dog is conscious, could evolve naturally without hundreds of millions of years of ancestral suffering. Pain is an indispensable component of the evolutionary process after organisms have reached a certain stage of complexity.[14]

Given the overall good of the natural world, I suggest that such suffering does not seem incompatible with God's goodness. (One's judgment about suffering in nature will, of course, vary to the extent that one recognizes morally relevant states of awareness or pain and suffering among non-human animals.)[15]

Some innocent suffering might be prevented by divine intervention, but van Inwagen and others have argued that multiple divine miracles would destabilize the natural world. Van Inwagen asks us to imagine a miracle-based world:

God, by means of a continuous series of ubiquitous miracles, causes a planet inhabited by the same animal life as the actual earth to be a hedonic utopia. On this planet, fawns are (like Shadrach, Meshach, and Abednego) saved by angels when they are in danger of being burnt alive. Harmful parasites and microorganisms suffer immediate supernatural dissolution if they enter a higher animal's body. Lambs are miraculously hidden from lions, and the lions are compensated for the resulting restriction on their diets by physically impossible falls of high-protein manna. On this planet, either God created every species by a separate miracle, or else, although all living things evolved from a common ancestor, a hedonic utopia has existed at every stage of the evolutionary process.[16]

While van Inwagen makes a good point against supposing that God should sustain a miracle-based world, I suggest that theists need to appeal to greater goods and powers that will ultimately address the problem of innocent suffering. Marilyn Adams thinks that God has the power and goodness to defeat the evils of the world by way of a relationship between creatures and Creator, begun in this life and continued in the next:

> The worst evils demand to be defeated by the best goods. Horrendous evils can be overcome only by the goodness of God. Relative to human nature, participation in horrendous evils and loving intimacy with God are alike disproportionate: for the former threatens to engulf the good in an individual human life with evil, while the latter guarantees the reverse engulfment of evil by good. Relative to one another, there is also disproportion, because the good that God *is,* and intimate relationship with Him, is incommensurate with created goods and evils alike. Because intimacy with God so outscales relations (good or bad) with any creatures, integration into the human person's relationship with God confers significant meaning and positive value even on horrendous suffering. This result coheres with basic Christian intuition: that the powers of darkness are stronger than humans, but they are no match for God.[17]

Adams further contends that assessing the problem of evil using only secular values (for example, pleasure is good, suffering is bad) obscures the broader claims about the Christian vision of God. If the God of Christianity exists, then in addition to secular values there may be superabundant values of incomparably great depth and power that can engulf and transform those damaged by evil. Only if we consider the possibility that there is an afterlife in which the innocent are healed, the lost found, and evil defeated, as suggested by Adams, can a theist fully reply to the skeptic. The point is not just the mere positing of an afterlife, but entertaining the possibility of a broader arena with values that do not merely offset the ills of suffering but that (as it were) *out-scale* the ills. This is also John Hick's position. He firmly upholds the goodness of God:

> What does that ultimate context of divine purpose and activity mean for Auschwitz and Belsen and the other camps in which, between 1942 and 1945, between four and six million Jewish men, women, and children were

deliberately and scientifically murdered? Was this in any sense willed by God? The answer is obviously no. These events were utterly evil, wicked, devilish and, so far as the human mind can reach, unforgivable; they are wrongs that can never be righted, *horrors which will disfigure the universe to the end of time,* and in relation to which no condemnation can be strong enough, no revulsion adequate. It would have been better—much, much better—if they had never happened. Most certainly God did not want those who committed these fearful crimes against humanity to act as they did. His purpose for the world was retarded by them and the power of evil within it increased. Undoubtedly He saw with anger and grief the sufferings so willfully inflicted upon the people of His ancient choice, through whom His Messiah had come into the world.[18]

And yet Hick insists that this vision is only possible in the context of an afterlife: "If this life, so creative for some but so destructive for many others, is all, then despair at the human situation as a whole is appropriate. Indeed if an all-powerful God has deliberately created a situation in which this present life, with all its horrors, is the totality of human existence, we should hate and revile that God's callous disregard for his/her helpless creatures."[19] For Hick and others, it is not good that there is evil. And if there is only this life, God is not good. D. Cohn-Sherbok agrees. He writes from a Jewish perspective:

> The essence of the Jewish understanding of God is that He loves His chosen people. If death means extinction, there is no way to make sense of the claim that He loves and cherishes all those who died in the concentration camps—suffering and death would ultimately triumph over each of those who perished. But if there is eternal life in a World to Come, then there is hope that the righteous will share in a divine life. Moreover the divine attribute of justice demands that the righteous of Israel who met their death as innocent victims of the Nazis will reap an everlasting reward. Here then is an answer to the religious perplexities of the Holocaust.[20]

Some Jewish theologians see the Holocaust as a definitive disproof of theism or at least the undermining of a theism that regards God as a provident ruler of history. Others hold that only a God of cosmic power can redeem those who died in the Nazi-led genocide. Another factor that needs to be considered is the conviction that God suffers in and with creation. The belief that God suffers or grieves over the evils of the cosmos is called passibilism. (The denial that God suffers is called impassibilism.)[21] Alvin Plantinga advances a passibilist understanding of God:

> As the Christian sees things, God does not stand idly by, coolly observing the suffering of his creatures. He enters into and shares our suffering. He endures the anguish of seeing his son, the second person of the Trinity, consigned to the bitter, cruel and shameful death on the cross. Some theologians claim that God cannot suffer. I believe they are wrong. God's capacity for suffering, I believe, is proportional to his greatness; it exceeds our capacity for suffering in the same measure as his capacity for knowledge exceeds ours. Christ was prepared to endure the agonies of hell itself; and God, the Lord of the universe, was prepared to endure the suffering consequent upon his son's humiliation and death. He was prepared to accept this suffering in order to overcome sin, and death, and the evils that afflict our world, and to confer on us a life more glorious than we can imagine.[22]

Such an understanding of God is very far from the bystander we imagined at the beginning of this chapter. As Richard Swinburne observes, understanding God as one who shares the burden of overcoming evil challenges the idea of God as a mere observer:

> A theodicist [one who argues that God is just, notwithstanding worldly evil] is in a better position to defend a theodicy such as I have outlined if he is prepared also to make the further additional claim—that God knowing the worthwhileness of the conquest of evil and the perfecting of the universe by men, shared with them this task by subjecting himself as man to the evil in the world. A creator is more justified in creating or permitting evils to be overcome by his creatures if he is prepared to share with them the burden of the suffering and effort.[23]

The conviction that God suffers with creation should prompt an addition to the question I formulated earlier in this chapter on the compatibility of evil with God's goodness. For God, all the evils of the Creation are not only against His will and nature, they are the object of God's suffering and hatred: God hates evil.

I conclude this section with a comment on Dostoyevsky. In *The Brothers Karamazov*, which contains one of the most powerful literary treatments of the problem of evil, Dostoyevsky points the way to addressing evil in the light of God's proximate love for the world. Father Zossima reports: "Much on earth is hidden from us, but to make up for that we have been given a precious mystic sense of our living bond with the other world, with the higher heavenly world, and the roots of our thoughts are not here but in other worlds.[24] This vision is upheld by many mystics, philosophers, and theologians in the theistic traditions and will be explored in the last three chapters.

The Hiddenness of God Objection

John Schellenberg has argued in multiple places that if the God of Christianity exists, then God would be more evident. In particular, there would be no person seeking a rich relationship with God who would not find it. Because God is not evident to those who seek Him, we have reason to believe that there is no God.[25] Schellenberg advances his thesis with two parables. Here is the first:

> Suppose your daughter, whom you dearly love, is in the grip of an erroneous picture as to what sort of person you are and what you intend in relation to her. No matter what you do in seeking to facilitate real contact . . . the response is only fresh resistance. . . . Now suppose that some way of instantaneously transforming her perspective is made available to you: if you press this button she will see you for who you really are and the snagged and tangled and distorted beliefs will rearrange themselves into a clear perception of the truth. . . . But suppose also that in facilitating a correct picture of who you are and what you intend in this way, you will

render it inevitable that your daughter make at least an initial choice in favor of a meaningful relationship with you—that is, her choice to do so will not be free in the sense we have been emphasizing. . . . Surely you will still do it, for you see that a free choice, yea or nay, . . . *isn't threatened thereby* . . . (Wouldn't any parent make the correct view available, even if the choice facing the child is then so obvious and attractive as not to be free, rather than having the child persist forever in her misunderstanding-based free choice? And what would be chosen by a perfectly loving God, the one who according to spiritual geniuses like Jesus of Nazareth never ceases to seek the lost sheep and to reveal to it a shepherd?)[26]

And here is Schellenberg's second parable:

You're a child playing hide and seek with your mother in the woods in back of your house. You've been crouching for some time now behind a large oak tree, quite a fine hiding place but not undiscoverable—certainly not for someone as clever as your mother. However, she does not appear. The sun is setting and it will soon be bedtime, but still no mother. Not only isn't she finding you, but, more disconcerting, you can't *hear* her anywhere: she's not . . . talking to you meanwhile as mothers playing this game usually do.

Now imagine that you start *calling* for your mother. Coming out from behind the tree, you call out her name, over and over again. But no answer. . . . So you go back to calling and looking everywhere: through the woods, in the house, down the road. Several hours pass and you are growing hoarse from calling. Is she anywhere around? Would your mother—loving and responsible parent that she is—fail to answer if she were around?[27]

These arresting thought experiments are open to challenge. In the first one, Schellenberg gives little or no attention to the possible goods involved in a person's life independent of the mother/parent figure and, by analogy, of God. In the first experiment, imagine that your child falsely believes that you are a gun-running, anti-environmental industrialist who is cruel to your labor force. Imagine further, however, that in rebellion against you, your child effectively undermines arms manufacturers and heads up a leading pro-environmental business group dedicated to fair labor laws. Still further, imagine that you have an overwhelming personality, and, if you could push the button, she would lose some of her passion and sink into a timid, more tepid pursuit of the good. Would you push the button then? I would not.

As for the parable of hide and seek, there is again no attention to the goods of growing up as one's own person. Schellenberg seems to suppose that the mother should be making herself known constantly. The analogy with God seems to be this: A good God, like a good mother, would not allow for there to be *any* time when God is not clearly evident to creatures. This seems, in my view, too strong a thesis. Most Christian theists believe that ultimately all persons will know of God either in this life or the next, so in the analogy we would have to imagine the mother eventually reappearing. But to expect the mother or God to be continuously evident seems overwhelming and does not allow for much human independence.[28] Alan Padgett comments:

> I find [Schellenberg's] conception of the love of God too narrowly paternal. Schellenberg's understanding of God is controlling, masculine and patronizing. God will ensure belief for his creatures because, after all, he knows best. A more rich and adequate understanding of God avoids the narrow "Father-Child" model for one of two lovers, a model found in Scripture, mystics, and some philosophers (Hegel, Buber, Levinas). God creates the world as Other to himself/herself, to approach the world as a Lover. The love of God, on this model, implies the occurrence of rational non-belief. For the Lover does not wish to impinge upon the freedom of the Beloved to reject the advances of the Lover; the Lover wishes the Beloved to be both fully mature, not always pressed against her or his long-term choices and character.[29]

Thus, Schellenberg's argument, he concludes, does not convince those with a more adult-friendly model of divine-human relationships.

The Vices of God

Consider a more recent version of the problem of evil, as advanced by the New Atheists. Richard Dawkins criticizes theism based on the portrayal of God in the Bible:

> The God of the Old Testament is arguably the most unpleasant character in all fiction; jealous and proud of it; a petty, unjust, unforgiving control-freak; a vindictive, bloodthirsty ethnic cleanser; a misogynistic, homophobic racist, infanticidal, genocidal, filicidal, pestilential, megalomaniacal, sadomasochistic, capriciously malevolent bully. . . . The oldest of the three Abrahamic religions, and the clear ancestor of the other two, is Judaism: originally a tribal cult of a single fiercely unpleasant God, morbidly obsessed with sexual restrictions, with the smell of charred flesh, with his own superiority over rival gods and with the exclusiveness of his chosen desert tribe.[30]

Dawkins's portrait requires a lengthy reply, but here I shall focus on his charge that the God of the Old Testament is vain and jealous.

If we think only of earthly rulers or human beings, the desire to be worshiped is the height of vanity. And for an earthly ruler to be jealous of any other ruler, his desire for our complete fealty seems also to be a matter of megalomania. But if we take seriously the biblical and subsequent theological identification by the Christian Platonists of God and goodness, matters change. If God is essentially good and the goods of the cosmos reflect God's goodness, then to worship God is to take delight in and respond in reverence and awe to goodness itself. Worship is not, then, paying compliments to a massive ego, but reverencing the goodness that makes created goods possible.

As for jealousy, God is depicted as jealous in the Bible. But is this always a vice? Imagine, again, that God is good and a relationship with God is itself good. What would be amiss if, say, a creature's desire for self-destruction aroused God to call this person back to a good life of harmony with God and this calling was out of jealousy? Assuming God to be the Creator of all, this would not be akin to a human being's. But even if we used human jealousy as an analogy or image of God's character, would this be a matter of vice? Imagine a healthy relationship between parents and a child until the child goes to college and becomes infatuated with an alcoholic, drug-pushing, pornography-watching, narcissistic philosophy professor whom the child calls "Daddy." Wouldn't the parents properly feel jealous and angry in response? The Old Testament portrait of a jealous God can be part of the biblical injunction to live fully and forsake violence: "Choose life in order that you may live" (Deut. 10:19). François Fénelon explicitly praised God's jealousy as a manifestation of the purity of divine love: "Nothing is so jealous, so severe, and so sensitive as this [divine] principle of pure love."[31]

Dawkins's failure to recognize the centrality of goodness in the Christian concept of God is made clear in his book *The God Delusion*. He defines what he calls "the God Hypothesis": "There exists a superhuman, supernatural intelligence who deliberately designed and created the universe and everything in it, including us. . . . Goodness is not part of the definition of the God Hypothesis, merely a desirable add-on."[32] But in the Christian Platonic tradition, goodness is the key reference point, the essential mark of divinity, and no mere "add-on" or afterthought. And this is also central to Judaism. The Old Testament offers a progressive or evolving portrait of God, beginning with a divine revelation to a nomadic "desert tribe" and then reaching out to the breathtaking dimensions of the great Hebrew prophets Isaiah and Jeremiah with their universal teachings of peace and justice. The key to answering Dawkins lies, in part, in taking seriously the theistic framework in which goodness is the central nature of God. [33]

Where Do We Go from Here?

Some of the treatments of the problem of evil stress the limitations of human resources to assess "the ethics of creation." What if, after sustained reflection, one does not see the point of creation; does it follow that it is pointless? A number of philosophers, called skeptical theists, challenge such an inference. Swinburne observes:

Note that the principle is so phrased that how things seem positively to be is evidence of how they are, but how things seem not to be is not such evidence. If it seems to me there is present a table in the room, or a statue in the garden, then probably there is. But if it seems to me that there is no table in the room, then that is the only reason for supposing that there is not, if there are good grounds for supposing that I have looked everywhere in the room, and . . . would have seen one if there was one there.[34]

Most theistic approaches to the problem of evil invite the long view. Hick is explicit on this point in the following passage, in which he contrasts "the great religions" with naturalism:

For quite apart from the sometimes tragic brevity of so many lives, even those who have lived the longest can seldom be said to have arrived, before they die, at a fulfillment of the human potential. We human beings are for so much of the time selfish, narrow-minded, emotionally impoverished, unconcerned about others, often vicious and cruel. But according to the great religions there are wonderfully better possibilities concealed within us. We see the amazing extent of the human potential in the great individuals, the mahatmas or saints, the moral and spiritual leaders and inspirers, and the creative artists of all kinds within every culture. We see aspects of it in innumerable more ordinary, but in some ways extraordinary, men and women whom we encounter in everyday life. We see around us the different levels that the human spirit has reached and we know, from our own self-knowledge and observation and reading, that the generality of us have a very long way to go before we can be said to have become fully human. But if the naturalistic picture is correct, this can never happen. For according to naturalism, the evil that has afflicted so much of human life is final and irrevocable as the victims have ceased to exist.[35]

Hick goes so far as to embrace a form of universalism in which all persons will be saved: "The least that we must say, surely, is that God will never cease to desire and actively to work for the salvation of each created person. He will never abandon any as irredeemably evil. However long an individual may reject his Maker, salvation will remain an open possibility to which God is ever trying to draw him."[36]

While not a universalist, Keith Ward holds a form of Christian theism according to which all creation will be transformed. Here is his poignant challenge to despair as well as a statement of Christian faith:

> One must remember that the Christian belief is that there is an existence after earthly life which is so glorious that it makes earthly suffering pale in comparison; and that such eternal life is internally related to the acts and sufferings of worldly life, so that they contribute to, and are essential parts of, the sorts of glory which is to come. The Christian paradigm here is the resurrected body of Jesus, which is glorious beyond description, but which still bears the wounds of the cross. So the sufferings of this life are not just obliterated; they are transfigured by joy, but always remain as contributory factors to make us the sort of individual beings we are eternally. This must be true for the whole of creation, insofar as it has sentience at all. If there is any sentient being which suffers pain, that being—whatever it is and however it is manifested—must find that pain transfigured by a greater joy. I am quite agnostic as to how this is to happen; but that it must be asserted to be true follows from the doctrine that God is love, and would not therefore create any being whose sole destiny was to suffer pain.[37]

This is a sweeping, serious vision of the defeat of suffering and evil. If Ward is right, then Hemingway's dictum cited in the introduction may be reversed: Madame, the best and truest story of creation, if continued long enough, ends in fullness of life. But let us get back to Strawson: is it an insult to God to believe or even to hope for this outcome? Let us consider in the next chapter how there might be a redemptive transformation.

CHAPTER 6

REDEMPTION AND TIME

God has also set eternity in their heart.
>   —Eccles. 3:11

I seek then to hear the voice which the dead are to hear,
and by which, having once heard, they shall live.
>   —Bernard of Clairvaux

I know some people who claim that they have no regrets in life at all. And Nietzsche has often been interpreted as claiming that redemption is achieved when a person wills (or accepts) his life just as it is (or has been). This idea is utterly foreign to me. While I do not spend ages in deep, stressful, agonizing regret, nevertheless, if I could turn back time, I would certainly change some things! These feelings are hardly unique. Some of the most profound expressions of regret take the form of someone claiming that *if they could change the past, they would*.

In the last chapter we addressed the general problem of evil. Now we need to look at the key to the Christian vision of overcoming evil, which involves the transformation of evildoers into persons who are redeemed, and the healing of damaged persons (either victims or agents) into a radically transformed union with God. This transition or radical shift raises questions about time and sequence. Unfortunately, from my point of view, the transition does not involve changing the past, but it does involve moving through and beyond the past.

The Stages of Redemption

Christian philosophers have, in general, been in broad agreement about many of the stages involved in redemption. Let's return to Pat and Kris's relationship with each other. Pat needs to confess the betrayal, show remorse, and ask Kris for forgiveness. On Kris's side, most Christian ethicists think that eventually Kris should forgive Pat and should welcome the restoration of the relationship. The "should" here is customarily treated not as a moral duty but as a fitting response. This preserves the idea that forgiveness is a gift, rather than a matter of contractual duty or something that can be coerced. Now let's focus briefly on forgiveness and punishment, and then move to a Christian account of redemption that enables there to be a union (atonement or at-one-ment) with God.

The standard definition of forgiveness is that one person forgives another when she either repudiates or moderates her resentment of someone who, she believes, has committed a wrong against her.[1] If she claims to forgive a wrongdoer but has no less resentment toward him, there has been no genuine forgiveness.

I am uneasy about whether this analysis cuts to the core of forgiveness. Couldn't someone forgive someone else and lack any resentment whatsoever? We may still want to say that the forgiver has *a right to feel resentment*, but perhaps she is incapable of doing so. Also, my reservation about the standard model stems, in part, from an uneasiness about "resentment" itself. Goethe defined it as impotent hatred, and, perhaps because of this, he recommended that we should not hate what we cannot destroy. *Resentment* seems to me to be a reactive mood: the resenter is brooding or smoldering. In any case, I offer an alternative.

When, say, Kris forgives Pat, then Kris also ceases to blame Pat for the wrong and does not let it stand in the way of restoring their relationship. But I propose that if I claim to truly forgive you for some wrong but continue to blame you for it (say, sending you text messages like "you were wrong"), then the forgiveness has yet to take place. In this relational thesis, one person forgives another person for a wrong act when she ceases to blame the other person for the act, and when she deliberately sets the act to one side in the hope for a future relationship.

Consider an objection: Imagine that Pat was unbearably cruel to Kris and remains unrepentant. Couldn't Kris still forgive Pat, even though Kris has no intention of having any positive relationship with Pat? I am inclined to think that this may involve genuine forgiveness on Kris's part, but it is incomplete or tarnished because of Pat's failure to repent. In any case, I offer you the relational thesis for your own reflection and further inquiry. Arguably, it is an ideal account, for in the real world we might genuinely forgive someone for some wrong, but either we or they may be so damaged that any future relationship would be more damaging rather than healing.

A few words need to be said on the notion of punishment before heading deeper into matters of redemption. There are abundant theories of when or if punishment is proper, how degrees of punishment should be determined, and who the proper agent(s) are who may inflict it. Leaving aside a host of issues, consider only two points. First, it is plausible to believe that most wrongdoing involves a person doing whatever he pleases despite a known moral prohibition. The wrongdoer may not have enjoyed the act or felt pleasure, but there remains the fact that he put whatever pleased him (or whatever he preferred) first. Punishment may be seen in such a case as actually or symbolically removing the pleasure. Punishment may be seen as a way of (as it were) wiping the smile off the face of the wrongdoer. In the course of punishment, a wrongdoer is not allowed to relish past stolen pleasures or to extract enjoyment from having done wrong in the past—or at least pressure is exerted to discourage him from doing so.

A second aspect of punishment is worth noting. We usually restrict the term "punishment" for juridical, institutional contexts and only use it metaphorically or poetically when referring to noninstitutional events, such as "the storm punished the ship," or "he got what he deserved" when, for example, a murderer is accidentally run over by a car. But in the Hebrew Bible's Old Testament, punishment can come by way of natural events (a flood) or by way of agents (an invading army) who have no concept of punishment. This aspect becomes relevant below.

Two Christian Models of Redemption

The context and challenge of reconciliation become enlarged when considering redemption and God. According to one popular understanding of redemption, long associated with Anselm of Canterbury, when persons do wrong or evil or sin, they not only wrong a fellow creature and themselves but they also wrong God, for God is the very source of goodness and, as the Creator of all, harming the creation counts as a violation of God's will and nature. Thus, such persons are deserving of punishment. In the New Testament the terms are severe: the wages of sin is death (Rom. 6:23). In mercy, God becomes incarnate as Jesus Christ, who lives a flawless life, shows us the ways of God, and then, in his passion and death, bears our sins. This suffering involves a vicarious death (dying for someone else) and a substitution (an innocent person standing in for the guilty one). There is great scriptural support for this understanding of redemption. Jesus is described as sinless and yet bearing the sins of the people (2 Cor. 5:21; John 1:29).

This model—sometimes called the Anselmian or juridical model—may seem counterintuitive: How can an innocent person be punished for the sake of a guilty one and the innocent person's death remove the rightful punishment for the guilty? We can, however, make some sense of how an innocent person may pay a debt or fine for another innocent person. The idea of an innocent person substituting himself for another is given a plausible shape, for example, in Charles Dickens's *A Tale of Two Cities*.[2] I believe the substitutionary model is coherent and profound, although here I want to explore an alternative model that reconceives what it was for Jesus to bear sins of others and that gives a greater role to Christ's death and resurrection in redemption, rather than treating Christ's death as the central, controlling instrument of redemption.

This alternative is the Christus Victor model, in which redemption involves Christ's victory over death.[3] On this view, humanity sins; and, in addition to human persons needing to be reconciled with one another, they need to be reconciled with God. The problem, though, is with time and power. Once you have harmed someone, you simply cannot go back and reverse the harm, as in the wrongful killing of a person. But even in less dramatic cases, restitution is difficult. If, as a college professor I break the Eleventh Commandment (Thou shalt not be boring), I can never give my students back the fifty-five minutes of class time that I wasted. In the Christus Victor model, all is not lost. God becomes incarnate as Jesus Christ, and his birth, life, teaching, miracles, passion, death, and resurrection have at least three roles.

First, Jesus is an exemplar, instructing us about God's will and nature and how we should live. This level of instruction is not simply by way of didactic instruction, where we conceive of Jesus as a super-professor. Rather, Jesus teaches by both word and example. While this stage or role in redemption is essential, it is deeply tied to the second role.

Second, Jesus embraces the human condition, including what may be considered the natural punishment of sin (death), and yet he overcomes death and promises life to all mankind through his resurrection. On the Anselmian model, Jesus' death is key. As Anselm puts the matter, "God became man, and by his own death, as we believe and affirm, restored life to the dead."[4] In a sense, while I cannot restore fifty-five minutes to my students or bring back to life someone whom I have killed, God through Christ can. On this view, Christ's bearing of sin amounts to Christ's bearing of the consequence—or, if you will, the punishment—involved in sin. Imagine an analogy: you have been leading a life of deliberate, wrongful outrageous dissipation. You are experiencing organ failure and loss of blood. You confess your wrongdoing, repent, but cannot (of your own power) mend. But then Christopher appears: he gives his own blood and indeed even organs to heal you. In so doing, he undergoes a suffering similar to the one you brought on yourself. In his life and example you observe a profound love for you. But, in the Christus Victor model we cannot leave the analogy with the death of Christopher. We have to go on to imagine that Christopher genuinely gave his life so that you may live (he dies) and then that Christopher passes from death to life. This may be supernaturalistic for some readers, but it is thoroughly in line with New Testament and Christian teaching about redemption and the resurrection. In scripture, Jesus identifies himself as the resurrection. In John 11:25, Jesus does not say "I am the crucifixion" or "I am death" but "I am the resurrection." To be sure, you cannot be resurrected unless you die, but in life and history, death is routine. It is the resurrection that is the good news.

And third, the Holy Spirit completes our union with Christ. The union with the Holy Spirit is crucial to this model since it functions to redeem the penitent by his adoption into God's life. In the process of redemption leading to atonement, he becomes a child of God.[5] This adoptive incorporation of the self into the divine God may be something that is dynamic and to be renewed (1 Cor. 14:16; Eph. 4:15; Phil. 1:21).

So, let's go back to Pat and Kris. An important element in this model is the need for the wrongdoer to utterly renounce the past error and thereby to die to his past life or identity. In Pauline language this is the death of the old Adam, and its chief realization in salvation history is the death of Christ (Rom. 6). We are to put away sin and then accept renewed life through his life, crucifixion, death, burial, and resurrection (Rom. 6:3; Gal. 2:19; Col. 2:13, 3:4). By identifying with the human condition, Christ assumes the awful results of sin (2 Cor. 5:21; Gal. 3:13), but what consummates the act is *restoration* through the resurrection.

This account of redemption is deeply Shakespearean. Especially in the comedies, redemption comes about by someone being brought to life who was either dead or believed to be dead. In *The Winter's Tale*, it appears that King Leontes has killed his wife, Queen Hermione. Only after lengthy mourning is he prepared for a reconciliation that occurs when Hermione comes back to life (she was only in hiding). In *Cymbeline*, Imogen seems to die and is restored, thus bringing her estranged husband, Posthumus, to repentance. In *As You Like It*, the evil brother Oliver repents after his good brother rescues him from death. In *Measure for Measure*, Angelo is restored after it is realized that the person whom he sought to execute has been restored. In *Pericles*, reconciliation occurs through Thaisa dying and then being brought back to life. Similar patterns of moving from apparent death to life may be seen in *Much Ado about Nothing, Twelfth Night*, and *A Comedy of Errors*. In some of Shakespeare's tragedies, evil befalls a main character because he cannot renounce his own evildoing (or, in a sense, die to his old self). In *Macbeth*, there is a brief moment when Macbeth contemplates reform but does not act on it. The same is true in *Hamlet*, when Claudius considers confession. These cases of unrepentant acts can be seen as those in which the character turns that which is living into something dead, as when Othello kills Desdemona in a jealous rage.

The Christus Victor model's role in some of Shakespeare's works stands in contrast to Stephen Davis's use of the Bard. Davis proposes that *Romeo and Juliet* would have been a farce if the Capulets and the Montagues had come to realize that their feud was pointless and were reconciled. Davis imagines that, after Tybalt's death, a stranger intervenes:

> "Wait, let me speak. Don't you realize that this feud is a bad idea? Think of all the people who have died and the people who could die today. Wouldn't it be better for the two families just to forgive and make up?"
>
> And then, simultaneously, the Lords of the two houses realize that this stranger is correct. "Yes," they say, each hitting himself in the head, "that's right. Why didn't we think of that? It *would* be better just to make up. Let's end the feud right here and now."
>
> And at that, there is a group hug of all the actors on stage; everybody goes home happy; and the curtain falls.[6]

Rather than such peacemaking, Davis writes: "Somebody had to die." He holds that we sinners deserve a torturous death; "the amends [for the offending party, us]—so it might seem—would be for each person to die on a cross in payment for his or her sins." Davis adds, "But the trouble with that idea is that it would accomplish nothing. It would be a meaningless death." His theology of substitution and sacrifice is bolstered by his appeal to Leviticus 16, Yom Kippur, and the following passage in Hebrews: "[W]ithout the shedding of blood, there is no forgiveness of sins" (Heb. 9:22). Davis summarizes his position:

In order to rectify it [our sin] an enormous cost had to be paid. God could not 'just forgive.' That would have been as pointless as fighting wars with robots or ending *Romeo and Juliet* with a group hug. A terribly wrong situation had to be set right. Somebody had to die. And the one who died was Christ. His blood paid the penalty for our sins. His death made possible the forgiveness of our sins. That was the price that had to be paid. Christ's death on the cross made possible our redemption. When our sins are forgiven, the iron wall is knocked down. The estrangement is over. We can have fellowship with God.[7]

But to return to my main point: the Christus Victor tradition upholds the fittingness of Christ's death and resurrection. In being put to death as an innocent person, Christ took on and bore the effect of sin, but this was undertaken because—reversing Davis's dictum—someone has to live. In *Much Ado about Nothing*, for example, the young soldier Claudio believes that he has been betrayed by the maiden Hero. On what was to be their wedding day, he repudiates her, causing her father to join with him in vile, annihilatory terms: "Hence from her! let her die" (Act 4, scene 1). This fits the "someone had to die" precept, and indeed, in the face of Leonato's violent condemnation ("O, she is fall'n / Into a pit of ink, that the wide sea / Hath drops too few to wash her clean again"), she appears to die. However, this is not the end. A good friar conspires with the aggrieved family and friends of Hero to make Claudio and the others believe that she had died. It then becomes clear that Hero, having been framed by villains, is innocent. Claudio repents, mourns, but is ultimately healed when "The former Hero! Hero that is dead!" (Act 5, scene 4) comes back to life, they are joyfully reunited, and the friar leads the couple to a chapel to be married.[8]

The saving role of the dying and rising Christ led some early Church theologians to see Jesus as the true Phoenix:

Let us consider the strange sign which takes place in eastern lands, that is, in the regions near Arabia. There is a bird called the phoenix. It is the only one of its kind and it lives for five hundred years. When the time for its dissolution in death approaches, it makes for itself a sepulchre of frankincense and myrrh and the other aromatics, into which, when the time is fulfilled, it enters and dies. From its decaying flesh a worm is born, which is nourished by the juices of the dead bird until it grows wings. Then, when it is strong, it takes up that sepulchre in which are the bones of the bird of former times, and carries them far from the land of Arabia to the city of Heliopolis in Egypt; and there, in the daytime, in the sight of all, it flies to the altar of the sun where it places them; and then it starts back to its former home. The priests then inspect the records of the times and find that it has come at the completion of the five hundredth year.

Do we, then, consider it a great and wonderful thing that the Creator of the universe will bring about the resurrection of those who have served Him in holiness and in the confidence of good faith, when He demonstrates the greatness of His promise even through a bird?[9]

Jesus, like the Phoenix, dies and rises, and we are called, too, to die to past sins to become a new creature (2 Cor. 5:17). Karl Barth took this model of regeneration very seriously, holding that in coming to Christ one literally becomes a new creature. Saved persons still remain human in this process or, as Barth put the point, the saved person "is still man and not cat!"[10]

What of those who do not know about Christ's redeeming work? Are they doomed to being perpetually unredeemed? This may not be due to any fault of their own. According to the Christus Victor model, the life and work of Christ are the means by which redeeming abundant life is made available for there to be a reconciliation or atonement of creatures and the Creator. But nothing about this model precludes the merits and power revealed in Christ's life, death, and resurrection being available to those who do not know Christ or even reject him as God incarnate. Either in this world or the next, the offer of abundant life may be revealed; and, assuming free will, perhaps only those who steadfastly and completely reject such abundant life will remain unredeemed. A failure of redemption is unfortunately not difficult to envisage. Imagine that I have done something horrific, such as wrongfully killing another man. Imagine further that he is miraculously brought back to life and I have an opportunity to be reconciled with him. But, rather than seeking atonement, I seize the opportunity to kill him again. Wouldn't refusal of life count as a kind of self-damnation?

Rather than conclude this sketch of the Christus Victor model with a double homicide, consider William Law's vision in 1728 of God's love and its central claim that this love will "raise all that is fallen":

> For to know that love alone was the beginning of nature and creature, that nothing but love encompasses the whole universe of things, that the governing hand that overrules all, the watchful eye that sees through all, is nothing but omnipotent and omniscient love using an infinity of wisdom to raise all that is fallen in nature, to save every misguided creature from the miserable works of its own hands, and make happiness and glory the perpetual inheritance of all the creation is a reflection that must be quite ravishing to every intelligent creature that is sensible of it. Thus to think of God, of providence, and eternity whilst we are in this valley and shadow of death is to have a real foretaste of the blessings of the world to come. Pray, therefore, let us hear how the letter of scripture is a proof of this God of love.[11]

Other Models

It may be useful to consider the credibility of the Christus Victor model by comparing it with several others. Two accounts involve thought experiments or parables. Consider first a parable advanced by one of my mentors, Philip L. Quinn:

> Imagine that a great magnate makes his two sons stewards of the two finest farms on his estate. The elder son irresponsibly neglects and thus ruins his farm, while the younger son conscientiously makes his farm flourish. As a result of his negligence, the elder son owes it to his father to make reparations by restoring his farm to its former prosperity. It would be severe but just for the father to punish him by disinheriting him if he does not repair the ruined farm. Unfortunately, the elder son is not a good enough farmer to be able to accomplish this task. . . . Acknowledging his responsibility

and guilt, the elder son repents of his negligence, and sincerely apologizes to his father. But the father . . . cannot help thinking that repentance and apology are not enough. . . . Moved by love for his brother as well as by devotion to their father and the welfare of his estate, the younger son undertakes to restore the farm that his brother has ruined to its former prosperity. . . . His guilty elder brother joins with him in this undertaking. And then a senseless tragedy occurs. At harvest time . . . marauding outlaws catch him [the younger son] in the open, slay him, and set the hay ablaze. His heroic attempt to restore the ruined farm ends in failure. But his sacrifices so work upon the grieving father's heart that he . . . mercifully refrains from exercising his right to disinherit his erring elder son.[12]

Quinn's thought experiment seems like a plausible account of how a Christ-like innocent brother might make a sacrifice that helps to bring about atonement. This parable is quite different from the Christus Victor model. In Quinn's story the death of the younger brother is "a senseless tragedy" rather than part of Christ's assuming the human condition, but this is a minor difference. The key difference is that there is no resurrection. The younger brother dies, whereas in the Christus Victor model, Christ dies to be resurrected and to promise resurrected life to others. The parable sees the saving work of the younger brother in terms of restoring to life that which was lost. I do not conclude that Quinn's parable is implausible or unfitting, but I suggest that the Christus Victor model speaks more effectively to the joy that Christians take in Christ's redeeming work.

Consider, now, Richard Purtill's thought experiment:

A certain king had a jewel which he valued so highly that he had enlisted a band of knights, sworn to safeguard the jewel or die in the attempt. An enemy of the king, desiring the jewel, corrupted the knights one after another, some with bribes, some with threats, and some with promises. Then the enemy carried off the jewel. The king's son, who had been away with his squire while this was happening, returned to find the jewel gone. He went alone into the enemy's stronghold and after great suffering, managed to get the jewel back. On his return the king held court. The foresworn knights came before him to express their sorrow and accept their punishment. The king's son was also there, and his father praised him for his heroism, promising him whatever reward he wished. The prince said to the king, "Father, as my reward I ask that you do not punish the foresworn knights. Let my sufferings in getting back your jewel be all that anyone has to suffer in this matter."[13]

This parable also seems to be a plausible case of an innocent person's suffering winning favor and atonement. It does have some demerits, however.

In Purtill's story, the innocent person's chief role is to placate the king. On the Christus Victor model the problem is one of restitution. Once I have harmed another person wrongly, I simply cannot restore the loss. Only God can pave the way for full restoration. The Christus Victor model thereby gives a more central and deeper role to the work of Christ. Also, on Purtill's model the jewel is the king's property, not a living thing, and its safekeeping is a matter of honor. The Christus Victor model sees the work of redemption not as the restoration of a valuable gemstone but as the restoration to life of those who die.

Incarnation and Time

Before we move on to the next chapter, "Eternity in Time," a modest observation: it seems that Christianity is committed to holding that God at least entered time through the Incarnation. I do not claim that this is incompatible with the view that God's very being (or God the Father) is atemporal, but it does involve God breaking into time as an incarnate person. The Incarnation may be seen as God's blessing the different stages of life and thus, in a sense, God's blessing of time. As Saint Irenaeus writes:

> He came to save all through Himself—all, I say, who through Him are reborn in God—infants, and children, and youths and old men. Therefore He passed through every age, becoming an infant for infants, sanctifying infants; a child for children, sanctifying those who are of that age, and at the same time becoming for them an example of piety, of righteousness,

and of submission; a young man for youths, becoming an example for youths and sanctifying them for the Lord. So also He became an old man for old men so that He might be the perfect teacher in all things—perfect not only in respect to the setting forth of the truth, but perfect also in respect to relative age—sanctifying the elderly and at the same time becoming an example to them. Then He even experienced death itself, so that He might be the firstborn from the dead, having the first place in all things, the originator of life, before all and preceding all.[14]

Just as the Incarnation has been seen as a blessing of time, it also has been seen as God's blessing the particularity and goodness of human flesh. The latter was a decisive reason why the early Christian church resisted Gnosticism, an early movement that regarded the body and the material world as evil.

Sometimes the particularity of the Incarnation has been regarded as embarrassing. The Roman philosopher Celsus (second century) ridiculed the idea that an all-good God would assume base matter as a body. But arguably it is the bodily specificity of the Incarnation that reminds one that Christian love must itself not get lost in generalities—think of a person who loves humanity as a whole or the idea of humanity but has trouble liking individuals.[15] Let us now move into eternity.

CHAPTER 7

ETERNITY IN TIME

Pay close attention to time, therefore, and
consider how you spend it; for nothing is more
precious than time. In one little moment, as
small as it may be, heaven may be won or lost.
—*The Cloud of Unknowing*

In the first chapter I referred to the claim by one of my graduate school
philosophy professors that "gravity is a manifestation of love" is obvious
nonsense. My project so far has been to build a case for a view of God
and the world that is distinct from that of contemporary naturalism and
materialism. We have not quite gotten to the place where gravity and love
are intertwined, in the spirit of Dante or the supposed nonsense example,
but we can now begin reflecting on the Christian thought and experience
that are like golden cords leading us to the eternal God.

I have a British friend who, when he is told of some catastrophe or
problems, usually responds with the line "I only work here." I get the im-
pression that my friend simply appears in our space-time universe from

time to time. Perhaps his attitude is helpful, and perhaps he does have supernatural powers, though I find myself more transfixed by moments in which our space-time universe seems to open up and allows us an encounter with something more, something that Cambridge Platonists and other Christians have described in terms of eternity. Such glimpses or encounters can be dramatic, as with Augustine and Monica, or quite ordinary. One of my most moving recent experiences that I would describe as an experience of the eternal consisted of feeling utterly in awe of an outpouring of compassion shown by a colleague for a friend who was battling cancer. The sky did not open and the colleague was not surrounded by flames, but I experienced it as transcendent and of everlasting value.

In this chapter, let us consider the Christian experience and reflection on God's eternity. Some Christian philosophers understand God to be timeless, others think of God as existing at each time, and still others think of God as temporal but in some sense the Lord of Time. As indicated in the introduction, this book does not take sides on this question. I want to look instead at the values that come into play when God is extolled as eternal. The bedrock of the great values involved in the experience of the eternal God is a sense of God's indwelling and a call to be drawn ever more deeply into the divine presence. Three features come to the fore. The experience of and reflection on God as eternal impel us, first, to subordinate or repudiate the pursuit of worldly glory (fame, power, prestige); second, to recognize that God is the God of irrepressible life; and third (the subject of my last chapter), to recognize the hallowed nature of domestic virtue.

Divine Indwelling and the Journey to God

Following Augustine and Aquinas, classical Christian theology claims that God is omnipresent through His power (all that exists is sustained by God's creative will), knowledge (God knows all of creation), and essence. That God is present where you are now means, in part, that God knows unsurpassably all that transpires where you are: God knows you thoroughly (there are no secrets hidden from God), and your being and all that is around you exists by virtue of His creative conservation. Some of us in the Platonic Christian tradition go further in also claiming that God is affectively responsive to the goods and ills of creation. So, insofar as you are engaging in something good, this may be understood as engaging in what pleases God. This is part of the passibilist tradition discussed in chapter 5. St. Gregory of Elvira describes God's ubiquity in colorful themes: "God is all eye, because He sees all; all ear, because He hears all; all mouth, because He is all Word; all tongue, because He speaks all; all foot, because He is everywhere; all hand, because He operates everywhere."[1] A passibilist would add: God is all heart, because God is affectively present everywhere.

But while classical theists affirm God's ubiquity, they have also distinguished cases of when God may or may not be said to dwell within the soul. As Augustine writes, "God is everywhere by the presence of his divinity, but not everywhere by the grace of His indwelling."[2] God's indwelling requires the open reception or consent of the creature. Once one is open to abiding in God, there is a kind of dual indwelling: the soul abides in God, and God abides in the soul. It is because of this abiding that many Christian mystics speak of finding rest in God, a Sabbath with no end (*tempus interminable*), a dynamic joy. In the classic *The Love of Learning and the Desire for God*, Jean Leclercq writes of the dynamic happiness to be found in abiding in God:

> All the most beautiful things, the most pleasing to the senses, to be found in the Scripture are called upon to give an idea of this total happiness: fruits, flowers, Springtime, sunlit meadows, the glory of the Saints, the splendor of the Lamb, the recovered harmony between flesh and spirit, health, inexhaustible youth, understanding and mutual love among the elect, unalterable union—nothing is lacking of all that the Christian could desire to receive from God upon entering the heavenly joys. But this happiness is not static, fixed once and for all within a boundary that cannot be crossed. Happiness grows to the degree that it receives satisfaction, and is satisfied in the proportion that it grows. Endlessly, desire and possession cause each other to increase, because God is inexhaustible—and this

consideration is, no doubt, the one which best helps us acquire a certain picture of what eternity really is. . . . The joys which more than satisfy the senses and the spirit seem to renew themselves, because the Lord gives of Himself more and more.[3]

This dynamic joy linking God and creatures, or the vision of such a joy to be anticipated, seems to be an element in the encounter with God as eternal, for the encounter involves values that are everlasting and enduring.

Before delving into the awesome goods relating to the experience of and reflection on God's eternity, I note that there are ways in which one's ultimate view about God being temporal or timeless can have an impact personally. Imagine that Pat is a presentist and believes that God exists in the present, while Kris believes God is atemporal and timeless. Both, I submit, can apprehend and appreciate divine indwelling and calling, as well as the three great goods explored in this and the next chapter. Both might well testify to the awesomeness of feeling God's presence, and both might think that they are wholly present to God. But for Pat, God's temporal ubiquity will not include past and future, because presentists hold that only the present exists.[4] Still, I submit that, for both of them, encountering God as eternal involves encountering an overwhelming wholeness, as opposed to a fragmented or splintered reality, and the essence or fountain of life itself. They can both lay claim to Boethius' thesis: "Eternity then is a full and perfect possession of the whole of everlasting life, altogether and at once," though for Pat the presentist there is an ongoing, ever-renewing divine life in which God is fully and perfectly the essence of life itself both now and in the future. On that point, Pat would have to treat Boethius' "at once" as something repeatable.

Both presentists and more traditional theists who regard God as atemporal can appreciate that the experience of God may subordinate our ordinary, metric experience of time to an experience of a kind of sacred moment, or what Charles Taylor refers to as "higher times." In *A Secular Age*, Taylor observes that the recognition of sacred days (Good Friday or Easter Sunday, for example) can lead us to feel, in the present moment, close to the sacred events themselves. Taylor puts the point this way:

Now higher times gather and re-order secular time. They introduce "warps" and seeming inconsistencies in profane time-ordering. Events which were far apart in profane time could nevertheless be closely linked. . . . Good Friday 1998 is closer in a way to the original day of the crucifixion than midsummer's day 1997. Once events are situated in relation to more than one kind of time, the issue of time-placing becomes quite transformed.[5]

While the traditionalist might think of the original Good Friday as still existing but at a specific point in the past, and the presentist thinks of the past *as no more*, both can appreciate experiences of transformation when the significance of an encounter with God at one moment leads one to weigh and view time from a kind of God's-eye point of view. Rather than (in Taylor's colorful phrase) finding ourselves "lost in our little patch of time," we find ourselves in a new, profound, divine setting.[6]

Transient and Eternal Goods

The classic in the Christian tradition on God's eternity, *The Consolation of Philosophy* by Boethius, can be read as a work of high philosophy inspired by Plato, Aristotle, and Plotinus. But, if read in this fashion, we can easily forget that this sixth-century text was written in a dungeon in Alvanzano, near Milan. It first and foremost warns us of the transience and seductive power of seeking worldly goods and reputations. Boethius had been a consul to Theodoric, king of the Ostrogoths. In 522, good fortune led to his two sons also being appointed consuls. The next year he was named *magister officiorum*, a close advisor to the king. But in 524, his good fortune utterly collapsed, and he was convicted of treason and executed in 525.

Boethius' meditation on divine eternity addresses some puzzles in philosophical theology, especially the quandary of reconciling God's omniscience and human freedom. If God knows now that you will, for example, donate clothes to a charity tomorrow, how could you do otherwise? Foreknowledge appears to fix the future. There are dozens of replies to this puzzle; Boethius' solution is to point out that if God is eternal, then He does not foreknow what will take place, because God is not in time. Your future is, as it were, present to God or, putting it differently, God is present to what we call the future:

> Why then do you demand that all things occur by necessity, if divine light rests upon them, while men do not render necessary such things as they can see? Because you can see things of the present, does your sight therefore put upon them any necessity? Surely not. If one may not unworthily compare this present time with the divine, just as you can see things in this your temporal present, so God sees all things in His eternal present. Wherefore this divine foreknowledge does not change the nature or individual qualities of things: it sees things present in its understanding just as they will result some time in the future. It makes no confusion in its distinctions, and with one view of its mind it discerns all that shall come to pass whether of necessity or not.[7]

Boethius' proposal (and variants of it) for reconciling omniscience and freedom has brilliant defenders today. But what many of his readers do not appreciate is his thesis that before God's eternal presence, all our ambitions for personal and worldly glory and success pale.

Boethius is asking us to consider what appears to be glory from the standpoint of divine everlasting wisdom and love:

> Kings you may see sitting aloft upon their thrones, gleaming with purple, hedged about with grim guarding weapons, threatening with fierce glances, and their hearts heaving with passion. If any man takes from these proud ones their outward covering of empty honour, he will see within, will see that these great ones bear secret chains. For the heart of one is thus filled by lust with the poisons of greed, or seething rage lifts up its waves and lashes his mind therewith: or gloomy grief holds them weary captives, or by slippery hopes they are tortured. So when you see one head thus labouring beneath so many tyrants, you know he cannot do as he would, for by hard task-masters is the master himself oppressed.[8]

Boethius is able to have this vision partly out of a sense of God's knowledge, goodness, and power.

Realizing that God knows *all* can be emancipating. It means that God knows all sorrows in the cosmos; God knows of your family, the children or spouse you once had, loneliness, imprisonment, injuries and successes, failed relationships, broken promises, and sustaining friendships. For Boethius, the simple thesis that there is a God who knows all would mean that Boethius' own particularly brutal execution would not go unwitnessed. A sense of God's goodness and power were also central to Boethius, for they ensured that death and annihilation are not the absolute end of the soul, and that the time for tyranny will end. His belief that the cosmos was created and is sustained for the good enabled him to see tyrants as dysfunctional or parasitic, misusing the talent and energy that are intended by the Creator to be used for the good. Boethius, like Augustine and Aquinas, held that power exercised in doing evil was not true or bona fide but the result of weakness—a failure to be wise, truly courageous, and just.

Perhaps it was Boethius' faith in God's power that consoled him when he was waiting for his execution. We may lose family, relations, and friends to estrangement and death, and yet God both knows of such losses and has the power to restore us. This thesis seems central to Augustine's understanding of God's eternal goodness. In *The City of God*, he consoles those who have faced heavy losses:

> And so there are indeed many bodies of Christians lying unburied; but no one has separated them from heaven, nor from the earth which is all filled with the presence of Him who knows whence He will raise again what He created. It is said, indeed, in the Psalm: "The dead bodies of Thy servants have they given to be meat unto the fowls of the heaven, the flesh of Thy saints unto the beasts of the earth. Their blood have they shed like water round about Jerusalem; and there was none to bury them." But this was said rather to exhibit the cruelty of those who did these things, than the misery of those who suffered them. To the eyes of men this appears a harsh and doleful lot, yet "precious in the sight of the Lord is the death of His saints."[9]

The same concern for values is at work in Augustine's *The City of God* and Boethius' *The Consolation of Philosophy* when eternal goods and temporal goods are compared.

In Book 1 of *The City of God*, Augustine contrasts the power and supreme goodness of humility over against imperial greatness:

> For I am aware what ability is requisite to persuade the proud how great is the virtue of humility, which raises us, not by a quite human arrogance, but by a divine grace, above all earthly dignities that totter on this shifting scene. For the King and Founder of this city of which we speak, has in Scripture uttered to His people a dictum of divine law in these words: "God resisteth the proud, but giveth grace unto the humble." But this, which is God's prerogative, the inflated ambition of a proud spirit also affects, and dearly loves that this be numbered among its attributes to "Show pity to the humbled soul, and crush the sons of pride."[10]

The last reference is from Virgil, the imperial poet who is valorizing Roman conquests. According to Augustine, Rome's vast achievements are subordinate to the merits and work of Christ. Such a subordination recognizes that while Christ's life and work took place in time, it has significance for all times and in all places. This is part of what some theologians have meant in claiming that the atonement revealed in Christ is eternal.

In *God Was in Christ*, D.M. Baillie links the historical event of Christ's life and redeeming work with God's merciful love. On this account, Christ's life, death, and resurrection did not cause God to have mercy on sinners; rather, God's merciful love was *the cause behind (and hence antecedent to) the Incarnation and act of redemption in time.* Baillie goes so far as to refer to the eternal, redemptive, sin-bearing love of God as atoning love. This is somewhat puzzling because atonement, as noted earlier, refers to a reconciliation, and one may well ask how there could be a divine-human reconciliation prior to there being humans. But there is scriptural precedent behind the notion that the gift of redemption was determined by God "before the world was made" (Eph. 1:3–14). As Saint Leo I taught, "It was in no new counsel nor by any tardy pity that God took thought of the situation of men; but from the foundation of the world He established one and the same cause of salvation for all. For the grace of God, by which the whole body of the saints is ever justified, was augmented, not begun, with the birth of Christ; and this sacrament of significations that those who believed its promise obtained no less than those who received its fulfillment."[11]

Baillie writes of the divine, *eternal* Atonement that is realized in time in Christ. And in Christ we see manifested what God wills always, even before the Incarnation. Christ's offering is identified as once for all in history:

> As God was incarnate in Jesus, so we may say that the divine Atonement was incarnate in the passion of Jesus. And if we then go on to speak of an eternal Atonement in the very being and life of God, it is not by way of reducing the significance of the historical moment of the Incarnation, but by way of realizing the relation of the living God to every other historical moment. God's reconciling work cannot be confined to any one moment of history. We cannot say that God was unforgiving until Christ came and died on Calvary; nor can we forget that God's work of reconciliation still goes on in every age in the lives of sinful men, whose sins He still bears.[12]

Emil Bruner held a similar idea, though he might have overstated it: "The Atonement is not history. The Atonement, the expiation of human guilt, the covering of sin through His sacrifice is not anything which can be conceived from the point of view of history. This event does not belong to the historical plane. It is super history, it lies in the dimension which no historian knows in so far as he is a mere historian."[13] I suggest that this might be overstatement because it is the temporal particularity of the Incarnation that allows us to recognize what early Christians saw as God blessing time and material bodies (a point I advanced in the last chapter). But the overall Baillie-Brunner thesis speaks to the Boethian and Augustinian point that all temporal, transient powers need to be (from a Christian point of view) subordinate to the everlasting, eternal redeeming life, work, death, and resurrection of Christ.

Before moving to the next dimension of value in the encounter with the eternal God, a further point needs to be made about Augustine's view of time. In the *Confessions*, Augustine gives ample space to reflections on the nature of time itself in a fashion that is philosophically fascinating. While acknowledging its intrinsic interest for the philosophy of time, however, I suggest that Augustine's central goal is discovering *God's presence* either in or beyond time as we know it. His conclusion that time is to be found in God generates a heightened sense that our measurement of time itself needs to be understood with reference to the mind of God:

> It is in my own mind, then, that I measure time. I must not allow my mind to insist that time is something objective. I must not let it thwart me because of all the different notions and impressions that are lodged in it. I say that I measure time in my mind. For everything which happens leaves an impression on it, and this impression remains after the thing itself has ceased to be. It is the impression that I measure, since it is still present, not the thing itself, which makes the impression as it passes and then moves into the past. When I measure time it is this impression that I measure. Either, then, this is what time is, or else I do not measure time at all.[14]

Augustine's work on time seamlessly leads him to reflect on time in the liturgy:

> It is not like the knowledge of a man who sings words well known to him or listens to another singing a familiar psalm. While he does this, his feelings vary and his senses are divided, because he is partly anticipating words still to come and partly remembering words already sung. It is far otherwise with you, for you are eternally without change, the truly eternal Creator of minds. In the Beginning you knew heaven and earth, and there was no change in your knowledge. In just the same way, in the Beginning you created heaven and earth, and there was no change in your action. Some understand this and some do not: let all alike praise you. You are supreme above all, yet your dwelling is in the humble of heart. For *you comfort the burdened*, and none fall who lift their eyes to your high place.[15]

For both Boethius and Augustine, reflections on God's eternity coax us to detach ourselves from worldly success and to not lose our souls in fragmented, conflicting desires. It is God's fullness of being that is key. Saint Gregory of Nazianzus uses a meditation on God's eternal fullness to humble human pretensions to knowledge:

> God always was and is, and will be; or better, He always is. *Was* and *will be* are portions of time as we reckon it, and are of a changing nature. He, however, is ever existing; and that is how He names Himself in treating with Moses on the mountain. He gathers in Himself the whole of being, because He has neither beginning nor will He have an end. He is like some great sea of Being, limitless and unbounded, transcending every conception of time and nature. Only His shadow falls across the mind, and even that but dimly and obscurely, as shadow produced not by what He truly is, but only by the things around Him, partial images gathered from here and there and assembled into one, some sort of presentation of the truth, but which flees before it is grasped and escapes before it is conceived.[16]

We are not thereby bidden to forsake the shadowy ideas we have of God, though we do well to realize that His fullness transcends our best ideas.

To summarize this first awesome good: a realization of God as eternal subordinates or exposes the vanity of the pursuit of worldly, temporal values. One of the central teachings in the Christian Platonic tradition is that the pursuit of worldly power and pride is empty from the standpoint of God's eternity, and we may and should be consoled when we realize the extent of the knowledge and power of this eternal God. The second awesome good that is part of the experience of the external God is the experience of God as the essence and source of all life.

God as the Essence of Boundless life

The literature on eternal life suggests that in the encounter with God, one encounters the foundation for the limitless fulfillment of created persons. This extraordinary testimony to God's eternal, life-giving power is extolled in the ecstatic ending of Saint Bonaventure's *The Tree of Life*, written in the thirteenth century:

From this Fountain [of life and light]
flows the stream of *the oil of gladness*,
which *gladdens the city of God*,
and the powerful fiery torrent,
the *torrent*, I say, *of pleasure* of God
from which the guests at the heavenly banquet
drink to joyful inebriation. . . .

Anoint us
with this sacred oil
and refresh
with the longed-for waters of this torrent
the thirsting throat of our parched hearts
so that *amid shouts of joy and thanksgiving*
we may sing to you
a canticle of praise. . . .[17]

In Bonaventure's poem, as well as in so much of the literature describing the experience of and reflection on God's eternity, one finds in God the essence of life itself. There is no other reality more alive, more plentiful in superabundant goodness. There is often a sense of God as self-generating, inexhaustible goodness and beauty. This seems to be at the core of Augustine's recognition of God as Beauty, ever new, and also the testimony of the poet R. S. Thomas, cited in the introduction, in which there is reference to "a young God." In *The Divine Names* of Denys the Areopagite, God is extolled as self-diffusive goodness; creation may be a free act of God, but it also is a natural outpouring of divine goodness. And in exercising God's generative creative power, there is no diminution of God's being. As Gregory of Nyssa writes, God is "always the same, never increasing or diminishing . . . standing in need of nothing else, alone desirable, participated in by all but not lessened by their participation."[18]

Perhaps one way to highlight the experience of God's inexhaustible, self-diffusive goodness is to compare the opposite experience. There are few books better than Charles Williams's *Descent into Hell*, which narrates a character's descent into a meaningless void. Lawrence Wentworth goes through experiences that are the mirror opposite of Thomas's. He is an ambitious, selfish historian who is given over to petty professional jealousy, a frightening lust, and self-deception. Gradually he loses the good of his mind and community, and, in the end, he is surrounded by baffling shapes: "There was, at the end of the grand avenue, a bobbing shape of black and white that hovered there and closed it. As he saw it there came on him a suspense; he waited for something to happen. The silence lasted; nothing happened. In that pause expectancy faded. Presently then the shape went out and he was drawn, steadily, everlastingly, inward and down through the bottomless circles of the void."[19] Expectancy is enhanced for finding insurmountable life.

One other text worth pausing over to sketch the opposite of the experience of God's eternity as boundless life is Christopher Marlowe's play *Doctor Faustus*. The devil Mephistophilis describes hell to Dr. Faustus in terms of a deprivation of everlasting bliss: "[W]hy this is hell, nor am I out of it. / Think'st thou that I, who saw the face of God, / and tasted the eternal joys of heaven, / am not tormented with ten thousand hells / In being deprived of everlasting bliss?"[20] In this succinct vision, hell is a deprivation, an inversion of the intoxicating joy expressed by Bonaventure.

In Faustus' final speech before his damnation, there is a searing sense that because he has repudiated the eternal God, time itself has become an enemy:

O, Faustus,
Now hast thou but one bare hour to live,
And then thou must be damned perpetually.
Stand still, you ever-moving spheres of heaven,
That time may cease, and midnight never come.
Fair nature's eye, rise, rise again and make
Perpetual day. Or let this hour be but a year,
A month, a week, a natural day,
That Faustus may repent and save his soul.
The stars move still, time runs, the clock will strike.
The devil will come, and Faustus must be damned.

Being unable to stop time, Faustus wrestles until the last instant with his folly.

> O, I'll leap up to heaven; who pulls me down?
> One drop of blood will save me.
> Rend not my heart, for naming of my Christ.
> Yet will I call on him. O spare me, Lucifer.

> Let Faustus live in hell a thousand years,
> A hundred thousand, and at last be saved.
> No end is limited to damned souls.

> *The clock strikes twelve.*
> It strikes, it strikes! Now body turn to air,
> Or Lucifer will bear thee quick to hell.
> O soul be changed into small water drops,
> And fall into the ocean ne'er be found.

> *Thunder, and enter the devils.*
> O mercy, heaven! Look not so fierce on me;
> Adders and serpents let me breathe awhile.
> Ugly hell, gape not; come not Lucifer!
> I'll burn my books! Oh, Mephistophilis! *Exeunt.*[21]

Unlike Goethe's Faust, Marlowe's Faustus seems damned even when he is still alive, and he becomes increasingly desperate with each passing moment as he moves from life to death.

There is a vast chasm between Marlowe's tragic protagonist and Bonaventure's portrait of the soul devoted to God. Two features of the experience of God's boundless life should be highlighted: first, the way in which the experience of God as the essence of life leads the soul to naturally long for and love God; and, second, the impact of this love for the belief in the life beyond this one. Indeed, the conviction that we are naturally drawn to the love of God is especially evident in Christian meditations on the Song of Songs, the Old Testament erotic love poem, which many Jewish and Christian mystics have interpreted as depicting the love affair between God and the soul.

The magnifying quality of God's love involves the soul's coming to share the power of divine love. One way to spell this out is by appreciating the general precept that if something is good (compassion, virtue, justice, wisdom), then to love the good object is itself good. For example, compassion is good, and there is an additional, expanded good when compassion is loved. In this respect, goodness is different from material properties: to love a horse or the color blue is not to be a horse or blue. But with goodness, as with beauty and wisdom, there is a diffuse power in which the love of beauty and the love of wisdom are themselves beautiful and wise. A similar, darker outcome occurs with some vices: if you love cruelty, you are yourself (in some respects) cruel even if you never behave cruelly.[22]

In the Christian Platonic tradition the love of God is itself divine insofar as the love is itself what God wills and involves the affective joining of God and creature, for no love of God goes unrequited. The vital importance of God's desire for our love (that is, of reciprocation) is powerfully argued for by Sor Juana Inés de la Cruz in her theological works. A creature's love of God will always meet an antecedent love of God for the creature. Also, insofar as God is superabundant beauty, goodness, and wisdom, the love of God will itself be marked by divine beauty, goodness, and wisdom.

Kierkegaard offers this profound portrait of how human and divine love can be interwoven and magnified:

> When we say, 'Love saves from death,' there is straightway a reduplication in thought: the lover saves another human being from death, and in entirely the same or yet in a different sense he saves himself from death. This he does at the same time; it is one and the same; he does not save the other at one moment and at another save himself, but in the moment he saves the other he saves himself from death. . . . But the lover is not thereby forgotten. No, he who in love forgets himself, forgets his sufferings in order to think of another's, forgets what he himself loses in order lovingly to consider another's loss, forgets his advantage in order lovingly to look after another's advantage: truly, such a person is not forgotten. There is

one who thinks of him, God in heaven; or love thinks of him. God is love, and when a human being because of love forgets himself, how then should God forget him![23]

In Kierkegaard's vision, the God of eternal love blesses the lives of created persons.

As far as the afterlife goes, some contemporary Christian thinkers treat the traditional belief in life after death as a metaphor. D. Z. Phillips has endeavored to translate talk of eternity into talk about what is of ultimate importance. In his view, death is an annihilation of persons; there is no soul, and yet we can and should still retain much religious language about eternal judgment. Phillips seeks to advance his thesis in light of an experience he had in Poland in which the concept of "eternal judgment" has nothing to do with an afterlife:

> Warning of such an eternal judgment is given in the Gospels. I was privileged to be present on an occasion when I heard the warning delivered in a memorable sermon. It was in Warsaw, shortly before the Solidarity Revolution. I was attending a requiem mass for a student who had had his stomach kicked in by the police a year earlier. The police, of course, were not prosecuted. The doctors who tried, unsuccessfully, to save the student's life were too useful to prosecute. But the ambulance men . . . were given long prison sentences for criminal negligence. It was said that they had killed the student by the improper way they had lifted him and carried him to hospital. I shall never forget the opening words of the priest's sermon . . . 'Let us pray for murderers. Our brother is with the Lord. But there are those who are walking about with murder in their souls. What a terrible state to be in! Let us pray for murderers.' The authority in these words comes from their being the judgment which talks of pity and punishment at the same time. The most pitiful and terrible thing would be for the murderer not to repent before death.[24]

When the priest proclaimed that "our brother is with the Lord," he meant it. Most, or at least many, Christians would believe the priest when he contends that the student has not perished everlastingly but is with the

God of life who conquered death through Christ. Origen gives expression to the experience of God as life itself when he writes: "What sort of life shall we live when we are no longer living under the shadow of life but are in life itself?"[25] Phillips's concept of "eternity expressed in time" does not speak to the great experience of the eternal God in Christian tradition, who brings us ultimately into Origen's "life itself." One way to bring out the shortcoming of Phillips's position is this thought experiment: Imagine that Phillips deeply loved the student and that he had it in his power to save him. Wouldn't he use this power? Now, imagine that there is a God of limitless power and love. Wouldn't such a God save the student from perishing everlastingly?

I suggest, in light of the Christus Victor model defended in the last chapter, that the absence of life beyond this one would amount to the absence or failure of redemption and atonement. Some goods seem viable only for limited or intermittent periods. An exciting conversation, say, no matter how deep, profound, and mind-expanding will eventually reach a point when the participants want a break. But our concept of being a person is different. Can one ever exhaust the good of being a person? I suggest that our very concept of a person capable of multiple experiences, acts, and loves is (in reference to and in response to God's love) an irrepressible good; there is a glory to Bonaventure's vision of a perpetual delight in the vivifying powerful love of God. Origin gives expression to the experience of God as life itself when he writes: What sort of life shall we live when we are no longer living under the shadow of life but are in life itself?

Living with Eternal Life

Bonaventure's extolling God as the fountain of life securely locates God as the source and the chief reference point in how to live. Fountains and wells have been rich metaphors in Christian mystical tradition. It is by Jacob's well that Jesus taught the Samaritan woman about eternal life (John 4). And Abraham's servant acts rightly by a well and finds a wife for Isaac (Gen. 24), whereas Saul behaves dishonorably. One of the key elements in thinking of eternal life in terms of a fountain or a well came home to me during a recent conference on meditation in world religions.

At the conference there were representatives of Hindu, Buddhist, Jewish, Islamic, Quaker, and Christian traditions. Each person spoke movingly and sometimes autobiographically. But one man, who is now a Sufi, described his "spiritual journey" in a way that I found difficult. He claimed to have once been a Buddhist, then a Hindu, then an evangelical Christian, then a Daoist, and then finally a Sufi. He described himself as digging a series of "shallow wells." Only when he came to identify himself as a Sufi did he dig "a deep well."

I suggest that with Christianity and the other faith traditions, including Sufism, it is helpful to realize that the well or fountain is already there. An inquirer may, as it were, try to drink from a fountain or let down a bucket into a well and be disappointed, but there is no need to picture oneself as actually digging wells. Indeed, if Bonaventure is correct, then the water is already there for the drinking.

In the Gospel of John, Jesus said to the Samaritan woman at the well: "Every one who drinks of this water will thirst again; but whoever drinks of the water that I shall give him will never thirst; the water that I shall give him will become in him a spring of water welling up to eternal life" (John 4:13, 14). This portrait of abundance stands in contrast to Johannes Tauler's fourteenth-century warning:

> Surely, these are the cisterns from which nothing wells up from the ground, from which everything flows away as quickly as it came. What may pass for religion in these people is nothing but a set of methods and practices of their own choice. They do not turn to their ground; they have neither desire nor thirst for what is profound and never go below the surface. As long as they have fulfilled their outward observances, they are thoroughly satisfied. The cisterns they have made for themselves suit them fine, and for God they do not thirst. And so they go to sleep at night, and they rise again in the morning to their old routine, with which they are well pleased. But by adhering to the cisterns which they have dug for themselves in such a blind, cold, and hard way, they leave the fountains of living water untouched.[26]

CHAPTER 8

GLORY AND THE HALLOWING OF DOMESTIC VIRTUE

All our life is a festival: being persuaded that God is
everywhere present on all sides, we praise him as we till
the ground, we sing hymns as we sail the sea, we feel his
inspiration in all that we do.

—Clement of Alexandria

Now I behold as in a mirror, an icon, in a riddle, life eternal,
for that is naught other than that blessed reward wherewith
Thou never ceasest most lovingly to behold me, yea, even the
secret places of my soul. With Thee, to behold is to give life.

—Nicholas of Cusa

Consider G. K. Chesterton's delightful account of divine reveling in the context of his study of the works of Charles Dickens. Nothing could be further from the dinner party of Woolf's *To the Lighthouse*. I cite Chesterton at length:

To every man alive, one must hope, it has in some manner happened that he has talked with his more fascinating friends round a table on some night when all the numerous personalities unfolded themselves like great tropical flowers. All fell into their parts as in some delightful impromptu play. Every man was more himself than he had ever been in this vale of tears. Every man was a beautiful caricature of himself. The man who has known such nights will understand the exaggerations of [Dickens's] "Pickwick." The man who has not known such nights will not enjoy "Pickwick" nor (I imagine) heaven. For, as I have said, Dickens is, in this matter, close to popular religion, which is the ultimate and reliable religion. He conceives an endless joy; he conceives creatures as permanent as Puck or Pan—creatures whose will to live æons upon æons cannot satisfy. He is not come, as a writer, that his creatures may copy life and copy its narrowness; he is come that they may have life, and that they may have it more abundantly. . . . He is there, like the common people of all ages, to make deities; he is there, as I have said, to exaggerate life in the direction of life. The spirit he at bottom celebrates is that of two friends drinking wine together and talking through the night. But for him they are two deathless friends talking through an endless night and pouring wine from an inexhaustible bottle.[1]

A. E. Taylor offers a similar portrait of how one might, in time, encounter a kind of divine atemporality or at least a welcome detachment from our particular "patch of time" and a reclining and enjoyment of the present:

At a higher level than that of mere animal enjoyment, such as we may get from basking before a good fire, or giving ourselves up to the delight of a hot bath, we know how curiously consciousness of past and future falls away, when we are, for example, spending an evening of prolonged enjoyment in the company of wholly congenial friends. The past may be represented for us, if we stay to think of it at all, by whatever happened before the party began, the future—but when we are truly enjoying ourselves we do not anticipate it—by what will happen when the gathering is over. The enjoyment of the social evening has, of course, before and after within itself; the party may last two or three hours. But while it lasts and while our enjoyment of it is steady and at the full, the first half-hour is not envisaged as past, nor the third as future, while the second is going on. It is from timepieces, or from the information of others, who were not entering into our enjoyment, that we discover that this single "sensible present" had duration as well as order. If we were truly enjoying ourselves, the time passed, as we say, "like anything."[2]

This sense of timeless, unhurried consciousness resonates, for example, with T. S. Eliot's *Four Quartets* and is the mirror opposite of the dinner party in *To The Lighthouse*.

In this final chapter I propose that the eternality of God is closely related to the glory of God in the Platonic Christian tradition and the hallowing of domestic virtue. The two are deeply interwoven, because it is part of the divine glory to hallow domestic virtues. Before looking into divine glory, however, we must take seriously pagan glory.

On the topic of pagan glory, I have a confession: When I was a boy, I used to have a peculiar daydream about dying a heroic, but ignominious, hideous death. In one scenario I would come across a truck that had accidentally caught on fire, with a child in the front seat. I would somehow rescue the driver and the child and yet in the process be utterly disfigured by the burning fuel. I would perish quietly, unrecognizable, as I handed the child unharmed to his mother.

The root cause of this fantasy was a vain effort to achieve what the ancient Greeks referred to as *kleos*, or glory. For Homer, glory was a bloody affair and was often won on the battlefield. Holding up the blood-stained armor of a foe brought you glory—a mixture of fear and awe in the praise of others. In the *Iliad* and Herodotus' *History*, one finds examples of *kleos* in dying well in a heroic last stand: Hector fell before his beloved city of Troy while seeking to defend it, and his life historically has been taken as a monument to glory amid failure. Similarly, in one of the most famous last stands in history, Leonidas and his Spartans won *kleos* as they fought to the last man in the Battle of Thermophylae to stem the great Persian invasion.

Worldly glory or *kleos* has had enormous, seductive power. It was, in part, the desire for glory that led Athens into its tragic war with Sparta in the Peloponnesian War, a conflict that nearly brought Athens to the point of annihilation. Alexander the Great and Julius Caesar saw themselves as bearers of *kleos* or glory, and the quest for glory was kept alive after the collapse of the Roman Empire in the West. The court of Charlemagne celebrated his deeds in battle in the twelfth-century *Chanson de Roland*. And such modern empires as Britain, Spain, and Napoleonic France sought that blend of fear and exultant awe in praise and self-glorification. Such pagan glory is quite distant from the idea of glory in the New Testament and in much Christian spirituality.

Eternal Love in Ordinary Life versus *Kleos* in the Classics

The birth of Christianity mounted a challenge to pagan *kleos*. In the Incarnation, the eternal God of creation takes on human flesh and assumes the role of a servant (Phil. 2:7). In the ancient Greco-Roman world, a servant was almost always a nonentity. Although a servant or a slave may have had some status as a teacher, physician, or secretary, the vast majority were nameless (from the standpoint of Greco-Roman chronicles) and insignificant as individuals. The very idea that the external God of the cosmos might become incarnate as a servant was a revolutionary one. It was, of course, politically volatile, for it meant that those who were subordinate to the elite classes (the inheritors of wealth and power by birth) might be as important as their masters. It also meant that the ordinary tasks of life should be viewed in a new light. Should the aristocratic elite rethink their view of the labor of a farmer or merchant or those condemned to working in the mines? Christianity was slow to develop a radical critique of slavery or servitude, but it did inaugurate a reconceiving of the ordinary and domestic. In pagan Greco-Roman culture, the domestic was subordinate to glory. As Charles Taylor has argued in *A Secular Age*, Christianity involved recognizing the sacredness of ordinary, domestic life. *Kleos* can still rightly be seen in heroic conflict—Saint George can and should kill a dragon; Saint Anthony can and should fight demons in the desert; and Joan of Arc really was inspired by God to enable the coronation of Charles VII of France. But the overall teaching and ethos of Christian tradition are to recognize the good of raising children, of cooking food, of making love within a framework of commitment (Arthur and Guinevere, yes; Guinevere and Launcelot, no), of education, farming, dancing, and so on. This blessing of ordinary life by the eternal God adds to the powerful critique advanced by Boethius of the vanity of seeking worldly power and reputation.

There is a homeliness in the New Testament, in which one meets fishermen, tax collectors, prostitutes, adulterers, and ordinary soldiers, as well as rulers. The blend of the ordinary and extraordinary has been beautifully articulated by Eric Auerbach in his reflections on the arrest of Jesus and his betrayal by Peter:

> A tragic figure [Peter] from such a background, a hero of such weakness, who yet derives the highest force from his very weakness, such a to and fro of the pendulum, is incompatible with the sublime style of classical antique literature. But the nature and the scene of the conflict also fall entirely outside the domain of classical antiquity. Viewed superficially, the thing is a police action and its consequences; it takes place entirely among everyday men and women of the common people; anything of the sort could be thought of in antique terms only as farce or comedy. Yet why is it neither of these? Why does it arouse in us the most serious and most significant sympathy? Because it portrays something which neither the poets nor the historians of antiquity ever set out to portray: the birth of a spiritual movement in the depths of the common people, from within the everyday occurrences of contemporary life, which thus assumes an importance it could never have assumed in antique literature. . . . What considerable portions of the Gospels and the Acts of the Apostles describe, what Paul's Epistles also often reflect, is unmistakably the beginning of a deep subsurface movement, the unfolding of historical forces. For this, it is essential that great numbers of random persons should make their appearance.[3]

Here, Auerbach has captured the acute ways in which Christian theism affirmed the extraordinary in the ordinary. The kind of spirituality that celebrates the domestic as well as the eternal can be seen in such seventeenth-century manuals as *The Practice of the Presence of God* by Brother Lawrence and Jean-Pierre de Caussade's meditations on "the holiness of the present moment."

In Brother Lawrence's work, an everyday, ordinary spirituality is extolled in which the soul lives in God's presence through an ongoing single attention:

> I have since given up all forms of devotions and set prayers except those which are suitable to this practice. I make it my business only to persevere in his holy presence wherein I keep myself by a simple attention and a general fond regard to God, which I refer to as an *actual presence* of God. Or, to put it another way, an habitual, silent, and secret conversation of the soul with God. This often causes me to have feelings of inward rapture—and sometimes outward ones! They are so great that I am forced to have to moderate them and conceal them from others. . . . My most useful method is this simple attention, done with a passionate regard toward God to whom I find myself often attached with greater sweetness and delight than that of an infant at its mother's breast. So much so that—if I dare use this expression—I choose to call this state the bosom of God because of the inexpressible sweetness which I taste and experience there.[4]

In a complementary fashion, de Caussade beautifully praises God in the present as part of an ever renewed attendance upon the duty at hand:

> God's order and his divine will is the life of all souls who either seek or obey it. In whatever way this divine will may benefit the mind, it nourishes the soul. These blessed results are not produced by any particular circumstance but by what God ordains for the present moment. What was best a moment ago is so no longer because it is removed from the divine will which has passed on to be changed to form the duty to the next. And it is that duty, whatever it may be, that is now most sanctifying for the soul.[5]

My favorite case of blending domestic life with spiritual rigor is the work of Sor Juana Inés de la Cruz. In a letter written from her convent in Mexico City, she offers some excellent advice:

> What could I tell you, my Lady, of the secrets of nature that I have discovered while cooking? I observed that an egg unifies and fries in butter or oil, but to the contrary dissolves in syrup; that in order to keep sugar liquid it suffices to throw on it a very little bit of water flavored with quince or another bitter fruit; that the yolk and white of the same egg when separated and combined with sugar have an opposite effect, and one different from when they are both used together. I do not mean to tire you with such foolishness, which I only recount to give you a complete picture of my nature and because I think it will amuse you. But, my Lady, what can women know except philosophy of the kitchen? Lupercio Leonardo has said it well: it is possible to philosophize while preparing dinner.[6]

Part of the legacy of Christian tradition is finding glory in ordinary life among ordinary people, seeing golden cords in ordinary conditions that suggest the overarching eternal love of God.[7]

One suggestive visual representation of the Christian, hallowed nature of domestic virtue may be found in bodegón painting, a genre of art that reflects the Cambridge Platonist spirituality permeating this book. (As it happens, this style of painting flourished around the same time as the emergence of Cambridge Platonism.) The term *bodegón*, used to distinguish seventeenth-century Spanish still-life painting, typically refers to paintings of food and drink and other items from the pantry. The iconography in this usage of the term points to something very different, for example, from the historically significant still-life style called *nature morta*, which can function as a remembrance of death and the transience of all earthly pleasures. (Think of *momento mori*, the Latin phrase for *Remember your mortality*, sometimes translated with more candor as *Remember you will die*.) The Spanish bodegón paintings are more of a remembrance of life than of its earthly end, hinting at an abundant sacred life beyond and surrounding the ordinary activities of eating and living. Such paintings provide a visual expression of the Cambridge Platonist thesis: our transient but good life points to a greater, fuller life that surrounds and upholds this one.

Four Golden Cords

Let us consider four golden cords that can lead us "in at Heaven's gate, built in Jerusalem's Walls." Three are well known. The first blends romantic love and a sense of the divine; the second is a golden cord in the midst of profound evil; the third, a golden cord found in a time of serenity; and the fourth, a golden cord that undermined my boyhood fantasy about achieving worldly glory.

For the first golden cord, consider Dante's meeting with Beatrice one day in Florence in 1283. The poet Dante was eighteen years old, and Beatrice was only a few months younger. Dante describes seeing her in the company of two other women.

> As they walked down the street she turned her eyes toward me where I stood in fear and trembling, and with her ineffable courtesy, which is now rewarded in eternal life [Beatrice died at the age of twenty-four], she greeted me; and such was the virtue of her greeting that I seemed to experience the height of bliss. It was exactly the ninth hour of the day when she gave me her sweet greeting. As this was the first time she had ever spoken to me, I was filled with such joy that, my senses reeling, I had to withdraw from the sight of others.[8]

And yet, as Dante put it, "from that time forward love fully ruled my soul." He confessed: "If at that moment someone had asked me a question, about anything, my only reply would have been: 'Love.'"[9]

One lesson to draw from the Dante-Beatrice episode is that of receptivity. If Dante had not been open to "Love" in that moment, there would have been no transport of delight that would eventually inspire him to write one hundred cantos testifying to the sovereignty of love over all things. "My will and my desire were turned by love," writes Dante at the end of the *Divine Comedy*, "The love that moves the sun and the other stars."[10]

In his *The Figure of Beatrice*, Charles Williams offers an engaging look at how a person can embody or channel a divine power while at the same time remaining herself. Williams captures this dual role in the last words below, "This also is Thou, neither is this Thou":

> Beatrice was, in her degree, an image of nobility, of virtue, of the Redeemed Life, and in some sense of Almighty God himself. But she also remained Beatrice right to the end; her derivation was not to obscure her identity any more than her identity should hide her derivation. Just as there is no point in Dante's thought at which the image of Beatrice in his mind was supposed to exclude the actual objective Beatrice, so there is no point at which the objective Beatrice is to exclude the Power which is expressed through her. But as the mental knowledge or image of her is the only way by which that other Power can be known, so she herself is (for Dante) the only way by which that other Power can be known—since, in fact, it was known so. The maxim of his study, as regards the final Power, was: "This also is Thou, neither is this Thou."[11]

The meeting with Beatrice, or perhaps Beatrice as Dante imagined her, became a golden cord leading to the composition of the *Divine Comedy*, a work that may itself constitute a golden cord.

For the second golden cord, consider Saint Maximilian Kolbe, a Polish Franciscan who underwent martyrdom in the Nazi concentration camp of Auschwitz in Poland. Rather than the Beatrician vision blending romantic and eternal love, this is a case in which divine goodness is shown in the ugliest, most vile, and depraved of conditions. In the late 1930s when war broke out, Kolbe provided shelter for over three thousand refugees from Greater Poland (including two thousand Jews) in his friary in Niepokalanów. He was arrested and sent first to the horrific Pawiak prison in Warsaw, where he was repeatedly beaten for his professed faith in God, and then sent to Auschwitz. There are multiple eyewitness accounts of both the physical abuses he endured and the extraordinary ways in which he ministered to his fellow prisoners during the summer of 1941.

In July, three prisoners escaped; in reprisal, ten from these men's barracks were sent to the Bunker, an underground starvation cell, and thus to their eventual deaths. Kolbe offered to take the place of one of the ten, who had cried out in despair for his wife and children. Bruns Borgowiec, an interpreter in the Bunker, was an eyewitness to Kolbe's last days:

> Since [the prisoners] had grown very weak, prayers were now only whispered. At every inspection, when almost all the others were now lying on the floor, Fr. Kolbe was seen kneeling or standing in the centre as he looked cheerfully in the faces of the SS men. Two weeks passed in this way. Meanwhile one after another they died, until only Fr. Kolbe was left. This the authorities felt was too long; the cell was needed for new victims. So one day they brought in the head of the sick quarters, a German, a common criminal named Bock, who gave Fr. Kolbe an injection of carbolic acid in the vein of his left arm. Fr. Kolbe, with a prayer on his lips, himself gave his arm to the executioner. Unable to watch this I left under the pretext of work to be done. Immediately after the SS men with the executioner had left I returned to the cell, where I found Fr. Kolbe leaning in a sitting position against the back wall with his eyes open and his head dropping sideways. His face was calm and radiant.[12]

The heroism of Fr. Kolbe went echoing through Auschwitz. In that desert of hatred he had sown love. Indeed, Jerzy Bielecki, another eyewitness, declared that Fr. Kolbe's death was "a shock filled with hope, bringing new life and strength. . . . It was like a powerful shaft of light in the darkness of the camp." Amid the utter despair of the concentration camp, it was a great golden cord. This line from the account of his death stands out with awesome simplicity and force: "It was then that the unexpected had happened, and that from among the ranks of those temporarily reprieved, prisoner 16670 had stepped forward and offered himself in the other man's place."[13]

For the third golden cord, consider again the poet and vicar of Aberdeen, R. S. Thomas. In his poem "The Bright Field," Thomas describes how a moment's experience of a natural setting hints at the need and calling to a greater experience of the eternal: "I have seen the sun break

through / to illuminate a small field / . . . and gone my way / and for-
gotten it. But that was the pearl / of great price, the one field that had /
treasure in it."[14] Thomas's imagery recalls two parables of Jesus in Matthew: "The kingdom of Heaven is like treasure hidden in a field, which
someone found and hid; then in his joy he goes and sells all that he has
and buys that field. Again, the kingdom of heaven is like a merchant in
search of fine pearls; on finding one pearl of great value, he went and
sold all that he had and bought it" (Matt. 13:44–45; NRSV). Here,
Thomas is perhaps reminding us that in routine, anxiety, and mere "hur-
rying" we can sometimes miss out on our encounter with the eternal.
There may be certain places where a meditative openness can draw us
out of ourselves.

By way of filling out the experience Thomas speaks to, it is worth
considering the final lines in C. S. Lewis's *Reflections on the Psalms*:

> The external may meet us in what is, by our present measurements, a
> day, or (more likely) a minute or a second; but we have touched what
> is not in any way commensurable with lengths of time, whether long or
> short. Hence our hope finally to emerge, if not altogether from time (that
> might not suit our humanity), at any rate from the tyranny, the unilinear
> poverty, of time, to ride it, not to be ridden by it, and so cure that always
> aching wound ("the wound man was born for") which mere succession
> and mutability inflict on us, almost equally when we are happy and when
> we are unhappy. For we are so little reconciled to time that we are even as-
> tonished at it. "How he's grown!" we exclaim, "How time flies!" as though
> the universal form of our experience were again and again a novelty. It is
> as strange as if a fish were repeatedly surprised at the wetness of water. And
> that would be strange indeed; unless of course the fish were destined to
> become, one day, a land animal.[15]

Both Thomas and Lewis are commending the golden cord that can bring
us to the eternal God of life.

The fourth golden cord is personal and relates to my pathetic boyhood fantasy about glory. I was attending a church service one day with
my mother when I noticed a woman whose hands were badly scarred.

Later my mother explained, "She left two of her children in her car when she ran a quick errand. When she returned to her horror, she saw that the car had caught fire. Her hands were badly burned when she rescued both children." The self-offering of the mother, undergoing disfiguration and willing to give up her life for her children, filled me with awe. The mother was probably completely unself-conscious about her sacrifice, whereas I would have been the opposite. Her act was an act of love for her children; mine would have been an act for *kleos*.

Love, Love, Love.

I end this short book with reflections on the link between eternity and divine glory. Judaism, Christianity, and Islam challenged pagan glory by shifting our attention to the glory of God. Awe and praise are owed principally to God rather than to emperors and empires, warriors and athletes, conquerors and magistrates. In Christianity there is a traditional argument for God's triune nature that holds that God is perfect in love. In order to be perfect in love, He must embody self-love, the love of one person for another, and the love of two persons for a third. Arguably, self-love is essential for the other two loves. The Second Commandment ("You shall love your neighbor as yourself") presupposes self-love. As an example of love for another and love for a third (albeit a third object rather than a third person), consider the two great Romantic poets William Wordsworth and Samuel Coleridge. When they were young they loved each other (platonically) and they also loved a third, the English language. Together and separately they were inspired to great heights of achievement. And it was only when vanity overcame Wordsworth, and opium and self-doubt crippled Coleridge, that they faltered.

The Christian Trinity also may be seen as three persons with self-love; there is the love between Father and Son, and the love of both Father and Son for the Holy Spirit.[16] If God is timeless, then these three loves are atemporally eternal. If God is temporal, then these loves are continuous and renewed in the present. The worship of God—on either model—amounts to a delight in the highest loves and, ideally, would unite us with what God Himself loves. As the Cambridge Platonist Ralph Cudworth proclaimed in the seventeenth century,

> No man is truly free, but he that has his will enlarged to the extent of God's own will, by loving whatever God loves, and nothing else. Such a one does not fondly hug this and that particular created good thing, and enslave himself to it; but he loves everything that is lovely, beginning at God, and descending down to all his creatures, according to the several degrees of perfection in them. He enjoys a boundless sweetness, according to his boundless love. He enclasps the whole world within his outstretched arms; his soul is as wide as the whole universe, as big as yesterday, today, and forever.[17]

This vision is continuous in New Testament sources such as 1 Corinthians 13 and also in Clement's first-century declaration:

> Who is able to explain the bond of the love of God? Who is equal to the telling of the greatness of His beauty? The height to which love lifts us is unutterable. Love unites us to God. Love covers a multitude of sins. Love endures all things, is long-suffering in everything. There is nothing vulgar in love, nothing haughty. Love makes no schism; love does not quarrel; love does everything in unity. In love were all the elect of God perfected; without love nothing is pleasing to God. In love did the Master take hold of us. For the sake of the love which he had for us did Jesus Christ our Lord, by the will of God, give His blood for us, His flesh for our flesh, and His life for our lives.[18]

Clement's views provide a sharp contrast to ancient *kleos*. Rather than being won by killing an enemy on the field of battle, glory is won by Christ's self-offering, the shedding of his blood, and the Resurrection, that there might be renewed life.

Now, let me add two caveats in closing. First, nearly all Christian mystics and those who have reflected and defended Christian mysticism agree that moral theology and practice is antecedent to mysticism. One cannot reasonably pursue the relationship with the eternal God of love while living a lie, rancorous and unjust. A longer book on eternity would require a deeper treatment of the ethics of character. Here, I merely cite a twelfth-century text, Richard of St. Victor's *The Twelve Patriarchs*, that insists that primacy must go to moral theology over mystical theology. Richard likens moral theology to Leah and mystical theology to Rachel in the Genesis story of Jacob, who loves and desires Rachel but first, as demanded by her father, must marry Leah.

> Those who have been taught by experience rather than by hearing easily recognize how often it happens that Leah is substituted when Rachel is hoped for. . . . For what do we call sacred Scripture except the bedchamber of Rachel, in which we do not doubt that divine wisdom is hidden beneath the veil of attractive allegories? Rachel is sought in such a chamber as often as spiritual understanding is sought out in sacred reading. But so long as we are incapable of penetrating sublime things, we do not find the long-desired, diligently sought Rachel. . . . On the contrary, this divine reading frequently makes us aware of our foulness and pricks our hearts with compunction, when we consider it while we are unwilling and even seeking something else in it. Therefore, as often as we find compunction rather than contemplation in divine reading, without doubt we have found not Rachel but Leah in the bedchamber of Rachel.[19]

Second, many Christian mystics testify that the journey to the eternal God must pass through a "dark night of the soul," the *noche obscura*. John of the Cross is the true master of this path. And I highly recommend Nicholas of Cusa's *Learned Ignorance* as well as *The Cloud of Unknowing* on this ardent but difficult and arid passage of purgation and cleansing on the soul's journey.

But however arduous the moral training and the purgation of the soul, the endpoint of divine eternal glory is widely witnessed to in Christian experience and reflection as a kingdom of reconciliatory, redemptive, eternal loving joy. If there is any truth in such a vision, I suggest again that gravity may be a manifestation of love after all. It seems fitting to add that one of the great means of recognizing such love that moves the sun and the other stars—as universally testified to in Christian theology as a whole, not just the Platonic Christianity of this book—is humility. Saint John Climacus offers us the following sublime image:

> Humility is a heavenly waterspout which can lift the soul from the abyss up to heaven's height.
>
> Someone discovered in his heart how beautiful humility is, and in his amazement he asked her to reveal her parent's name. Humility smiled, joyous and serene: "Why are you in such a rush to learn the name of my begetter? He has no name, nor will I reveal him to you until you have God for your possession. To whom be glory forever." Amen.
>
> The sea is the source of the fountain, and humility is the source of discernment.[20]

In this exchange, by the divine sea, when she is asked about her parentage, I picture Humility laughing with a joy that welcomes you and me to join her.

NOTES

Introduction

1. *Ernest Hemingway: A Literary Reference*, ed. R. W. Trogdon (New York: Carroll and Graf, 2002), 158.

2. Jerry L. Walls, *Heaven: The Logic of Eternal Joy* (Oxford: Oxford University Press, 2002), 116.

3. Pierre Tielhard de Chardin, *Christianity and Evolution*, trans. René Hague (London: Collins, 1971), 112.

4. Thomas Nagel, *The View from Nowhere* (Oxford: Oxford University Press, 1986), 214.

5. Ibid., 209.

6. See Charles Carlton, *Going to the Wars: The Experience of the British Civil Wars, 1638–1651* (London: Routledge, 1993), esp. 209–10.

7. On current cosmology and Christian eschatology, see "The End of the World" by W. H. Craig, in vol. 1 of *Science and Religion in Dialogue*, ed. M. Y. Stewart (Oxford: Wiley Blackwell, 2010).

8. I do not claim that Cambridge Platonist writings directly influenced this group (known as the Inklings), only that their spirituality and the spirituality of the Cambridge Platonists bear a strong family resemblance.

9. Peter Sterry, "A Discourse of the Freedom of the Will," in *Cambridge Platonist Spirituality*, ed. Charles Taliaferro and Alison J. Teply (New York: Paulist Press, 2004), 179.

10. Virginia Woolf, *To The Lighthouse* (New York: Harcourt, 1955), 97.

11. Ibid., 111.

12. W. H. Auden, "The Protestant Mystic," in *Forewords and Afterwords* (New York: Random House, 1973), 69.

13. For an overview of Cambridge Platonism, see *Cambridge Platonist Spirituality*, ed. Taliaferro and Teply; W. R. Inge, *The Platonic Tradition* in *English Religious Thought* (New York: Longmans, Green and Co., 1926); *The Cambridge Platonists in Philosophical Context: Politics, Metaphysics, and Religion*, ed. G. A. J. Rogers et al. (Dordrecht: Kluwer, 1997); Benjamin Carter, *"The Little Commonwealth of Man": The Trinitarian Origins of the Ethical and Political Philosophy of Ralph Cudworth* (Leuven: Peters, 2011); and Charles Taliaferro, *Evidence and*

Faith: Philosophy and Religion since the Seventeenth Century (Cambridge: Cambridge University Press, 2005), chap. 1. It is gratifying to see one of the Cambridge Platonists, Henry More, included in a popular work, *Great Thinkers of the Western World*, ed. I. P. McGrell (New York: HarperResource, 1992). One of the greatest historians of ideas, Richard Popkin, pays More this somewhat guarded compliment: "Although More was not the most precise or consistent thinker of his time, he was one of the liveliest, wittiest, and satirical polemical writers of his day" (in *Great Thinkers of the Western World*, ed. McGrell, 203).

14. Ralph Cudworth, "A Sermon Preached Before the Honorable House of Commons at Westminster, March 31, 1647," in *Cambridge Platonist Spirituality*, ed. Taliaferro and Teply, 60.

15. Ibid.

16. William Blake, "Jerusalem," in *The Complete Poetry and Prose of William Blake*, ed. David V. Erdman, Harold Bloom, and William Golding (New York: Random House, 1988), 231.

17. Susan Blackmore, *Conversations on Consciousness: What the Best Minds Think about the Brain, Free Will, and What It Means to Be Human* (New York: Oxford University Press, 2006), 9.

18. George Orwell, "The Lion and the Unicorn," in *Why I Write* (New York: Penguin Books, 2005), 11.

19. For a brilliant defense of God's eternity as an atemporal reality, see Brian Leftow, *Time and Eternity* (Ithaca: Cornell University Press, 1991), as well as Paul Helm, *Eternal God* (Oxford: Clarendon Press, 1988); for the idea that God is in a "time beyond time," see R. M. Helm, "Some Reflections on the Neoplatonic View of Space and Time," in *Neoplatonism and Contemporary Thought*, ed. R. B. Harris (Albany: SUNY Press, 2002), 119–38. For a defense of God's temporality, see Richard Swinburne, *The Coherence of Theism*, 2d ed. (Oxford: Oxford University Press, 1993).

20. Tatian the Syrian, "Address to the Greeks," in *The Faith of the Early Fathers*, ed. and trans. W. A. Jurgens (Collegeville, MN: Liturgical Press, 1970), 1:66.

21. R. S. Thomas, as cited in *Threshold of Light: Prayers and Praises from the Celtic Tradition*, ed. A. M. Allchin and Esther De Waal (London: Dalton, Longman, and Todd, 2004), 15.

22. *Confessions of Saint Augustine*, trans. R. S. Pine-Coffin (New York: Viking Penguin, 1961), Book 10, p. 231.

23. One of the central elements in the Christian view of God's eternity is the boundless, inexhaustibleness of God's life. In my view, advocates of God's atemporality and those who believe that God is everlasting can claim to recognize God's perfect possession (*perfecta possessio*) of boundless life (*interminabilis vitae*), even if they disagree about whether this occurs in a never-changing instant—a state that is *tota simul*, without past or future—or whether God's life is ever new in the present. Whether I am correct in this proposal, however, is not the central topic of this book.

24. Wittgenstein's remark stands as a sharp contrast to Immanuel Kant, who referred to God as the most real being, *Ens Realissimum.*

25. Stendhal, *The Red and The Black*, trans. C. K. Scott-Moncrieff and R. Busoni (New York: Modern Library, 1929), 59.

26. Charles Taliaferro, *Love, Love, Love and Other Essays: Light Reflections on Love, Life, and Death* (Cambridge, MA: Cowley Publications, 2005).

27. I do not disparage apologetics. Indeed, one of the greatest early philosophical works is Plato's *Apology* on behalf of his teacher, Socrates. But my book is more of an exploration or extended essay than a work of systematic apologetics.

28. See my *Philosophy of Religion: A Beginner's Guide* (Oxford: One World Press, 2009), *Dialogues about God* (Lanham, MD: Rowman and Littlefield, 2009), and *Consciousness and the Mind of God* (Cambridge: Cambridge University Press, 1994). For a critique of naturalism and an implied, indirect defense of theism, see my *Naturalism*, co-authored with Stewart Goetz (Grand Rapids: Eerdmans, 2008).

Chapter 1. Love in the Physical World

1. Dante, *The Divine Comedy*, vol. 3, *Paradise*, trans. Dorothy L. Sayers and Barbara Reynolds (Harmondsworth: Penguin, 1962), 33.144–45 (p. 347).

2. Daniel Dennett, *Consciousness Explained* (Boston: Little, Brown, 1991), 33.

3. D. M. Armstrong, *The Nature of the Mental and Other Essays* (Ithaca: Cornell University Press, 1980), 1, 2.

4. Alistair Hannay, "The Claims of Consciousness: A Critical Survey," *Inquiry* 30 (1987): 397.

5. Stephen Stich. *From Folk Psychology to Cognitive Science: The Case against Belief* (Cambridge, MA: MIT Press, 1983), 229–30.

6. Paul Churchland, *Matter and Consciousness: A Contemporary Introduction to the Philosophy of Mind* (Cambridge, MA: MIT Press, 1984), 44.

7. Richard Rorty, "Mind-Body Identity, Privacy, and Categories," *Review of Metaphysics* 19:1 (1965): 30.

8. Jerry Fodor, "Is Science Biologically Possible?" in *Naturalism Defeated? Essays on Plantinga's Evolutionary Argument against Naturalism*, ed. James Beilby (Ithaca: Cornell University Press, 2002), 14, 30, emphasis Fodor's.

9. Peter Unger, *All the Power in the World,* (New York: Oxford University Press, 2006).

10. Daniel Dennett, "Facing Backwards on the Problem of Consciousness," in *Explaining Consciousness—the "Hard Problem,"* ed. Jonathan Shear (Cambridge, MA: MIT Press, 2000), 35, emphasis Dennett's.

11. Carl Sagan, *Cosmos.* (New York: Random House, 1980), 105.

12. Some philosophers think that the principle of the indiscernability of identicals runs into serious problems in the context of beliefs. To take the usual

example: you may know that the masked man robbed the bank, yet you do not know that your father robbed the bank. Supposedly, there is something true of your father, but (alas) it may turn out that the masked man is your father. The principle of the indiscernability of identicals is not violated, however. Imagine that your father *is* the masked robber. When you know that the masked man robbed the bank, the person who robbed the bank has the property of being recognized by you, the witness, as well as the property of being your father, though you do not yet recognize this additional, distinct property. Given the identity (robber = father), it remains the case that whatever is true of the one is true of the other: to pick out your father in a police lineup is to pick out the robber, to lock up your father in prison is to lock up the robber, and so on, even if not everyone grasps the identity.

13. Colin McGinn, *The Problem of Consciousness* (Oxford: Blackwell, 1991), 10–11.

14. Richard Swinburne, *The Evolution of the Soul* (Oxford: Clarendon Press, 1994), 147.

15. Daniel von Wachter, "What Kind of Modality Does the Materialist Need for His Supervenience Claim?" in *Irreducibly Conscious*, ed. A. Batthyany and A. Elitzur (Heidelberg: Universitätsverlag, 2009), 19.

16. Ibid., 8, 9.

17. Michael Lockwood, "Consciousness and the Quantum Worlds," in *Consciousness: New Philosophical Perspectives*, ed. Q. Smith and A. Jokric (Oxford: Clarendon Press, 2003), 447.

18. T. L. S. Sprigge, *The Importance of Subjectivity*, ed. L. B. McHenry (Oxford: Clarendon Press 2011), 50.

19. Charles Williams, *The Shadows of Ecstasy* (London: Faber and Faber, 1948), 36–37.

20. The use of a zombie thought experiment to challenge contemporary forms of materialism was first employed by David Chalmers. For an erudite overview of the literature, see Daniel N. Robinson, *Consciousness and Mental Life* (New York: Columbia University Press, 2008).

21. Daniel Dennett, *Brainstorms: Philosophical Essays on Mind and Psychology* (Montgomery, VT: Bradford Books, 1978), 72–73.

22. Georges Rey, *Contemporary Philosophy of Mind* (Oxford: Blackwell, 1997), 21, emphasis Rey's.

23. Dennett in Blackmore, *Conversations on Consciousness*, 87.

24. Dennett, *Consciousness Explained*, 29, emphasis Dennett's.

25. Paul Churchland, *The Engine of Reason, the Seat of the Soul* (Cambridge, MA: MIT Press, 1995), 8.

26. Ibid.

27. Richard Rorty, *Philosophy and the Mirror of Nature* (Oxford: Blackwell, 1980), 387.

28. Dennett, *Consciousness Explained*, 37.

29. Ibid.

30. Churchland, *The Engine of Reason*, 22.

31. Ibid., 8.

32. Ibid., 324.

33. Bertrand Russell, *An Outline of Philosophy* (London: Routledge, 1927), 78.

34. Noam Chomsky, "Naturalism and Dualism in the Study of Language and Mind," *International Journal of Philosophical Studies* 2 (1994): 195.

35. Though this is rarely noted, probably the first use of the term "materialism" was in the 1660s, by Cambridge Platonist Henry More.

36. H. H. Farmer, *God and Men* (London: Nisbet, 1948), 42–43.

37. Daniel Dennett, *Breaking the Spell: Religion as a Natural Phenomenon* (New York: Viking Press, 2006), 130.

38. Ibid., 239.

39. Dennett in Blackmore, *Conversations on Consciousness*, 88, emphasis Dennett's.

40. John R. Searle, *The Mystery of Consciousness* (New York: New York Review of Books, 1997), 112.

41. Thomas Nagel, "Conceiving the Impossible and the Mind-Body Problem," *Philosophy* 73 (1998): 344–45.

42. Ibid., 338.

43. Ibid., 351.

Chapter 2. Selves and Bodies

1. David Chalmers, *The Conscious Mind* (Oxford: Oxford University Press, 1996), 168.

2. Barry Stroud, "The Charm of Naturalism," in *Naturalism in Question*, ed. Mario de Caro and David Macarthur (Cambridge, MA: Harvard University Press, 2004), 22.

3. John R. Searle, *Mind: A Brief Introduction* (Oxford: Oxford University Press, 2004), 48.

4. Some philosophers believe that there can be contingent identities, but usually these identities do not involve strict references. For example, Barack Obama is the forty-fourth president of the United States, but this is not a necessary relationship, because the forty-fourth president might have been John McCain. If materialism is true, however, then what we refer to as Obama is strictly identical with what we refer to as his body. "The forty-fourth president of the United States" is a title that may be held by any number of people and is not a matter of strict reference.

5. Gilbert Ryle, *The Concept of Mind* (New York: Barnes and Noble, 1949), 11–12.

6. Ibid., 13, 20.

7. Dennett, *Consciousness Explained*, 37. While few would ever accuse Dennett of wallowing in mystery, in an essay on the status of nonhuman animal mental life, he seems unenthusiastic about removing the mystery concerning animal intelligence: "But perhaps we really do not want to know the answers to these questions [about animal consciousness]. We should not despise the desire to be kept in ignorance—are there not many facts about yourself and your loved ones that you would wisely choose not to know? . . . Learning all these facts would destroy my composure, cripple my attitude towards those around me. Perhaps learning too much about our animal cousins would have a similarly poisonous effect on our relations with them." While Dennett suggests that learning too much about animal minds might not be good, he also believes that we are underequipped philosophically to form a clear grasp of animal consciousness. See Daniel Dennett, "Animal Consciousness: What Matters and Why," *Social Research* (Fall 1995), available on the Internet under the heading "Dennett and Animal Consciousness."

8. Sallie McFague seems to link self-body dualism with arrogance, economism, anti-ecology, patriarchy, and so on. See, for example, her *Super, Natural Christians* (Minneapolis: Fortress Press, 1997).

9. I first defended integrative dualism in my *Conciousness and the Mind of God* (Cambridge: Cambridge University Press, 1994). The view is further developed in my "The Virtues of Embodiment," *Philosophy* 76:1 (2001): 111–25.

10. See the illustration by Taylor's (and my) professor Roderick Chisholm, in Richard Taylor, *Metaphysics* (Englewood Cliffs, NJ: Prentice Hall, 1974), 19.

11. David Rosenthal, "Dualism," in *Routledge Encyclopedia of Philosophy*, 1998, section 4. Published online.

12. This is a point that has recently been advanced by Derek Parfit in his two-volume work *On What Matters* (Oxford: Oxford University Press, 2011). This line of reasoning may also be found in a range of other writers, including C. S. Lewis, Robert Nozick, Victor Reppert, and Stewart Goetz.

13. See K. E. Himma,"What Is a Problem for All Is a Problem for None: Substance Dualism, Physicalism, and the Mind-Body Problem," *American Philosophical Quarterly* 42:2 (April 2005): 81–92.

14. Churchland, *Matter and Consciousness*, 20.

15. Robert Wald, *General Relativity* (Chicago: University of Chicago Press, 1984), 70. See also Robin Collins, "Modern Physics and the Energy Conservation Objection to Mind-Body Dualism," *American Philosophical Quarterly* 45:1 (2008): 31–42.

16. W. D. Hart, "Unity and Dualism," in *Irreducibly Conscious*, ed. Batthyany and Elitzur, 35.

17. Richard Swinburne, *The Coherence of Theism* (Oxford: Oxford University Press, 1993), 106–7.

18. For a detailed defense of this and other arguments for integrative dualism, see my articles: "Sensibility and Possibilia: A Defense of Thought Experiments,"

Philosophia Christi 3:2 (2002): 403–20; "Naturalism and the Mind," in *Naturalism: A Critical Analysis*, ed. W. L. Craig and J. P. Moreland (New York: Routledge, 2000); "Possibilities in Philosophy of Mind," *Philosophy and Phenomenological Research* 57:1 (1997): 127–37; "Animals, Brains, and Spirits," *Faith and Philosophy* 12:4 (October 1995): 567–81; and also my *Consciousness and the Mind of God*.

19. Peter van Inwagen, *God, Knowledge, and Mystery: Essays in Philosophical Theology* (Ithaca: Cornell University Press, 1995), 20.

20. For a detailed defense of this reply to van Inwagen, see my "Sensibility and Possibilia: A Defense of Thought Experiments."

21. Bernard Williams, *Problems of the Self* (Cambridge: Cambridge University Press, 1973), 11–12.

22. This argument is developed by Alvin Plantinga in "Materialism and Christian Belief," in *Persons: Human and Divine,* ed. Peter van Inwagen and Dean Zimmerman (Oxford: Clarendon Press, 2007), 99–141.

23. Søren Kierkegaard, *Works of Love,* trans. Howard V. Hong and Edna H. Hong (London: Wm. Collins Sons & Co., 1962), 76.

24. Someone may object: Consider the thesis that persons are modes of something greater, such as waves on the sea. Couldn't a person, like a wave, have sufficient distinctness to account for our sense that we love individuals? Possibly, though a wave has no independence of the water that makes it up. If persons are like a movement of water, rather than substantial individuals, it is hard to see how they would have any center or focus or selfhood. What would self-awareness be like in the view that you are a mode of a body? We can speak about waves having causal effects, such as the wave went over the seawall. But the wave is only an extension of the body of water itself.

25. Benjamin Whichcote, *Aphorisms*, cited by Ernst Cassirer in *The Platonic Renaissance in England*, trans. J. P. Pettegrove (Austin: University of Texas Press, 1953), 32.

26. *Paradise Lost*, Book 1. The idea that the mind or soul creates or gives shape to hell is also hinted at in Christopher Marlowe's play *Doctor Faustus*, in the famous line by the devil Mephastophilis, who tells Faustus that, despite appearances, Mephastophilis himself is not free of hell: "Why this is hell, nor am I out of it" (3.76–80).

Chapter 3. Some Big Pictures

1. Sterry, "A Discourse of the Freedom of the Will," in *Cambridge Platonist Spirituality*, ed. Taliaferro and Teply, 179–80.

2. For the record, I believe that Hobbes was (as he claimed) a theist, and so in that respect he is not the Dennett of the eighteenth century. Hobbes thought that God was a form of matter. He was suspicious of consciousness, however, and promoted a materialist, mechanistic model of the cosmos.

3. Matthew Bagger, *Religious Experience, Justification, and History* (Cambridge: Cambridge University Press, 1999), 15.

4. Ibid., 217.

5. Kai Nielsen, *Naturalism and Religion* (Amherst, NY: Prometheus Books, 2001), 279.

6. Ronald W. Hepburn, *Christianity and Paradox* (London: Watts, 1958), 5.

7. Gareth Moore, *Believing in God: A Philosophical Essay* (Edinburgh: T. & T. Clark, 1988), 17.

8. Jan Narveson, "God by Design?" in *God and Design,* ed. N. Manson (London: Routledge, 2003), 93–94.

9. Ibid., 94.

10. Brian O'Shaughnessy, *The Will* (Cambridge: Cambridge University Press, 1980), 1:xvii.

11. Leopold Studenberg, *Consciousness and Qualia* (Philadelphia: John Benjamins Publishing, 1998), 32.

12. Colin McGinn, *The Problem of Consciousness: Essays Towards a Resolution* (Cambridge, MA: Wiley-Blackwell, 1993), 47.

13. Richard Dawkins, *The God Delusion* (Boston: Houghton Mifflin, 2006), 149.

14. I borrow my subheading for this section from one of the great books in Muslim philosophy, *The Incoherence of the Incoherence,* written in the twelfth century by Ibn Rushd as a response to al-Ghazali's attack on philosophy called *The Incoherence of the Philosophers.*

15. Keith Ward, *Why There Almost Certainly Is a God* (Oxford: Lion, 2008), 79, 80.

16. Timothy O'Connor, *Theism and Ultimate Explanation* (Oxford: Blackwell, 2008), 82, 83.

17. John R. Searle, *The Re-Discovery of the Mind* (Cambridge: Cambridge University Press, 1992), 50, 51 (his emphasis).

18. Christian theologians have long noted that scriptural language of God is imperfect because of our limitations. Consider, for example, John Chrysostom's reference to condescension and weakness: "Do you see how all things were created by a word? But let us see what it says afterwards about the creation of man: 'And God shaped man.' See how, by means of a condescension of terms employed for the sake of our weakness, it teaches at the same time both the manner of creation and its diversity or variety, so that, speaking in human terms, it indicates that man was shaped by the very hands of God, even as another Prophet says: 'Your hands created me and shaped me.'" From John Chrysostom, "Homilies in Genesis," in *The Faith of the Early Fathers,* ed. Jurgens, 2:102.

19. A further defense of this thesis may be found in the treatment of Hume and Kant in my *Evidence and Faith.*

20. See the introduction, note 28.

21. I. A. Richards, *The Philosophy of Rhetoric* (New York: Oxford University Press, 1936), 65.

22. Some of these cases are addressed in my *Contemporary Philosophy of Religion* (Malden, MA: Blackwell, 1998).

23. See J. L. Mackie's *The Miracle of Theism* (Oxford: Clarendon Press, 1982), chap. 5.

24. For a further exposition, see Brian Leftow, "Necessity," in the *Cambridge Companion to Christian Philosophical Theology*, ed. C. Taliaferro and C. Meister (Cambridge: Cambridge University Press, 2010).

25. O'Connor, *Theism and Ultimate Explanation*, 70.

26. Augustine, *The Trinity*, in *The Faith of the Early Fathers*, ed. Jurgens, 3:76.

27. Daniel Dennett, *Darwin's Dangerous Idea* (New York: Simon & Schuster, 1995), 76.

28. R. Dawkins, *The God Delusion* (New York: Houghton Mifflin, 2006), 157–58.

29. Jil Evans, "Re-Imagine the Galapagos," in *Turning Images in Philosophy, Science, and Religion: A New Book of Nature*, ed. C. Taliaferro and J. Evans (Oxford: Oxford University Press, 2011), 233.

30. Ibid. See also Thomas Nagel, "Dawkins and Atheism," in his *Secular Philosophy and the Religious Temperament: Essays 2002–2008* (Oxford: Oxford University Press, 2010), 19–26, especially 22.

31. Daniel Dennett, *Breaking the Spell* (New York: Viking, 2006), 268.

32. See chap. 2, note 7.

33. See Darwin's treatment of races and extinction in *The Descent of Man*.

34. Julian of Norwich, *The Revelations of Divine Love*, trans. Elizabeth Spearing (London: Penguin Books, 1998), 7.

35. Jacques Maritain, *Integral Humanism*, ed. Otto Bird, trans. Joseph W. Evans, The Collected Works of Jacques Maritain, vol. 11 (Notre Dame: University of Notre Dame Press, 1996), 192.

36. Ernest Hemingway, *The Sun Also Rises* (New York: Simon & Schuster, 2002), 251. While citing Hemingway's novel to highlight resignation to the loss of a relationship, some Christian philosophers and theologians have used our sense of longing for completion (joy, happiness, home) as part of an extended argument that we are made for such a completion. In various places, C. S. Lewis has entertained what has been called the argument from desire, and J. R. R. Tolkien addresses this argument in his excellent essay "On Fairy-Stories." The philosophical theologian Ralph Harper wrote an extraordinary study of longing in his *Nostalgia: An Existential Exploration of Longing and Fulfilment in the Modern Age* (Cleveland: Press of Western Reserve University, 1966). In this genre, one of my favorite names for any argument is the "Factory Girl," as developed by Cardinal John Henry Newman. He imagines a factory girl who is thoroughly miserable but reasons that there has to be something better, a God who can and will bring healing. Newman argues that this can be a natural, legitimate inference. For an exposition and defense, see "Cardinal Newman's 'Factory Girl' Argument," *Proceedings of the Catholic Philosophical Association* 46 (1972): 71–77.

Chapter 4. Some Real Appearances

1. *Confessions of Saint Augustine*, trans. Pine-Coffin, Book 9, pp. 197–98.

2. In Goethe's *Faust II* the angels save the tragic "hero": "He who exerts himself in constant striving, / Him we can save." This may seem more like a valorization of ambition than seeking rest in the moment, but both *Faust I* and *II* are severe critiques of worldly ambition and glory. Moreover, in the scene of Faust's redemption, there is a restoration of that which is lost. The woman whom he had exploited and (indirectly) killed, Gretchen, is the one who welcomes Faust to a blessed afterlife. In the end, it is Faust's shedding his exhausting vainglory and resting in a fair moment that opens him up to eternity or, as Goethe puts it, to "The Eternal Feminine."

3. William Wordsworth, *Selections from William Wordsworth*, ed. A. H. Thompson (Cambridge: Cambridge University Press, 1917), 5.

4. Richard Bucke, *Spiritual Competency Resource Center*, http://www.spiritualcompetency.com/ (September 2009), 7–8.

5. Leslie Weatherhead, "The Christian Agnostic," quoted in Alistair C. Hardy, *The Spiritual Nature of Man: A Study of Contemporary Religious Experience* (Oxford: Clarendon Press, 1979), 53.

6. See, for example, William Alston, *Perceiving God* (Ithaca: Cornell University Press, 1991); Caroline Frank, *The Evidential Force of Religious Experience* (Oxford: Clarendon Press, 1989); Jerome Gellman, *Experience of God and the Rationality of Theistic Belief* (Ithaca: Cornell University Press, 1997); Gary Gutting, *Religious Belief and Religious Skepticism* (Notre Dame: University of Notre Dame Press, 1983); Richard Swinburne, *The Existence of God*, rev. ed. (Oxford: Oxford University Press, 1991); William Wainwright, *Mysticism: A Study of Its Nature, Cognitive Value and Moral Implications* (Madison: University of Wisconsin Press, 1981); Keith Yandell, *The Epistemology of Religious Experience* (Cambridge: Cambridge University Press, 1993); H. D. Lewis, *Our Experience of God* (New York: Macmillan, 1959); and Nelson Pike, *Mystic Union* (Ithaca: Cornell University Press, 1992).

7. See the excellent book *The Rainbow of Experiences, Critical Trust, and God: A Defense of Holistic Empiricism* by Kai-Man Kwan (London: Continuum, 2011).

8. See, for example, John Earman, *Hume's Abject Failure: The Argument against Miracles* (Oxford: Oxford University Press, 200).

9. Hume, "Of Miracles," in *An Enquiry Concerning Human Understanding*, 2nd ed., ed. L. A. Selby-Bigge (Oxford: Clarendon Press, 1902), 127–28.

10. Ibid., 110–11.

11. David Hume, "Of National Characters," in *The Philosophical Works of David Hume*, vol. 3, ed. T. H. Green and T. H. Grose (London: Longmans, 1886), 252. Unfortunately, Hume's position was not merely of academic interest. Hume's authority is appealed to and defended in such pro-slavery texts as the anonymously authored *Personal Slavery Established by the Suffrages of*

Custom and Right Reason (1773), Richard Nisbet's *Slavery Not Forbidden by Scripture* (1773), and Edward Long's three-volume racist text *The History of Jamaica*. And some anti-slavery works took issue with Hume: James Beattie's *Essay on the Nature and Immutability of Truth* (1770), and James Ramsey's *An Essay on the Treatment and Conversion of African Slaves in the British Sugar Colonies* (1784).

12. Sterry, "A Discourse of the Freedom of the Will," in *Cambridge Platonist Spirituality*, ed. Taliaferro and Teply, 181.

13. David Brian Davis, *The Problem of Slavery in Western Culture* (Ithaca: Cornell University Press, 1966), 351. Culverwel as well as Whichcote was a Cambridge Platonist.

14. Samuel Fleishacker, *Divine Teaching and the Way of the World* (Oxford: Oxford University Press, 2011), 26.

15. Ibid., 27.

16. Wesley Wildman, *Science and Religious Anthropology* (Burlington, VT: Ashgate, 2009), 25.

17. A brief word on behalf of skepticism: historically, skeptics about perception have had a decent track record ethically. In ancient Greece, few people doubted that slavery was a natural condition except for the skeptic Diogenes of Sinope (fourth century BCE). Between Plato and Aristotle, Plato was the more skeptical about the reliability of perception; Plato thought that we can often be victims of illusions. And yet it was Plato who had a higher view of women as potential political leaders than his contemporaries.

18. Wesley Wildman, *Religious and Spiritual Experiences* (Cambridge: Cambridge University Press, 2011), 160.

19. Ibid., 163.

20. For a classic study of religious experience, see Evelyn Underhill, *Mysticism* (Mineola, NY: Dover Publications, 2002), first published in 1911.

21. J. L. Schellenberg, *The Wisdom to Doubt: A Justification of Religious Skepticism* (Ithaca: Cornell University Press, 2007), 170–71.

22. Ibid., 172–74.

23. See Jeffrey Russell, *Inventing the Flat Earth: Columbus and Modern Historians* (New York: Praeger, 1997).

24. See Underhill, *Mysticism*. She offers a comprehensive, critical account of religious experience involving a broad range of cases.

25. Schellenberg, *The Wisdom to Doubt*, 183.

26. For a compelling case that one can observe oneself as an individual, substantial being, see Roderick Chisholm, "The Direct Awareness of the Self," in his *Person and Object: A Metaphysical Study* (La Salle, IL: Open Court, 1979).

27. It is hard to see how neurobiology could undermine religious experience without undermining much else. For a superb collection of essays on this topic, see *The Believing Primate: Scientific, Philosophical and Theological Reflections on the Origin of Religion*, ed. J. Schloss and M. Murray (Oxford: Oxford University Press, 2009).

28. For a detailed look at the arguments pro and con this objection and reply, see ibid., and J. Barrett, *Why Would Anyone Believe in God?* (Walnut Creek, CA: Alta Mira Press, 2004).

29. While I find such exchanges unhelpful in general, there is an excellent essay, "Is Religion Evil?" by Alister McGrath that effectively argues that Dawkins's claims about ethical atheism are naïve, in *God Is Great, God Is Good: Why Believing in God is Reasonable and Responsible*, ed. W. L. Craig and C. Meister (Downers Grove, IL: InterVarsity Press, 2009).

30. See Kai Man Kwan, "The Argument from Religious Experience," in *The Blackwell Companion to Natural Theology*, ed. W. L. Craig and J. P. Moreland (Oxford: Wiley-Blackwell, 2009).

31. For an excellent resource on recorded religious experiences, see Timothy Beardsworth, *A Sense of Presence* (Oxford: Religious Experience Research Unit, 1977). For two engaging and thorough, sympathetic treatments of the evidential value of religious experience, see John Hick, *The Fifth Dimension* (Oxford: One World Press, 2004), and his *The New Frontier of Religion and Science* (New York: Macmillan, 2006).

32. Peter Donovan, *Interpreting Religious Experience* (New York: Seabury Press, 1979), 81.

33. Norman Kemp Smith, "Is Divine Existence Credible?" in *Religion and Understanding*, ed. D. Z. Phillips (New York: Macmillan, 1967), 125. Of course, to a naturalist convinced of the falsehood of theism, living with the kind of openness to the presence of God commended by Donovan would not be like my examples involving animals and children, but more like an astrologer being open to discovering human destiny by studying the stars. Donovan's point and the position defended here are based on the thesis that theism, unlike astrology, is a live, credible, alternative to naturalism.

34. R. G. Collingwood, "The Devil," in *Religion and Understanding*, ed. Phillips, 189.

35. Jean-Paul Sartre, *Nausea,* trans. L. Alexander (New York: New Directions, 1964), 95–96. Sartre won and then turned down the 1964 Nobel Prize for literature for *Nausea*.

Chapter 5. Is God Mad, Bad, and Dangerous to Know?

1. I once presented a paper entitled "The World Is Not Enough" at several schools, arguing that an all-good God ought to annihilate creation. It is only due to God's goal of mercifully redeeming the wicked that God does not do what God ought to do if He acted on justice alone. On this view, divine mercy is in explicit tension with divine justice. I still believe this to be a coherent position and compatible with God's *goodness* as opposed to *justice*, but I will not defend this thesis here.

2. Erasmus, "Concerning the Immense Mercy of God," in *The Essential Erasmus*, trans. J. Dolan (New York: New American Library, 1964), 230.

3. Parfit, *On What Matters*, 1:267.

4. C. A. Campbell, *In Defense of Free Will* (London: George Allen and Unwin, 1967), 47.

5. Parfit, *On What Matters*, 1:269.

6. None of the characters in my story are real or resemble people I know.

7. Campbell, *In Defense of Free Will*, 47.

8. Gregory of Nyssa, *The Life of Moses*, trans. A. J. Malherbe and E. Ferguson (New York: Paulist Press, 1978), 2:3.

9. Sterry, "A Discourse of the Freedom of the Will," 181.

10. Ibid.

11. Catherine of Siena, *The Dialogue*, trans. S. Nofke (New York: Paulist Press, 1980), 37–38.

12. Goodness might well be seen as built into the animal world as well. George MacDonald once suggested: "The bliss of the animals lies in this, that, on their lower level, they shadow the bliss of those—few at any moment on the earth—who do not 'look before and after and pine for what is not' but live in the holy carelessness of the eternal *now.*" *George MacDonald: An Anthology,* ed. C. S. Lewis (London: Geoffrey Bles, 1955), 114.

13. Holmes Rolston III, "Does Nature Need to be Redeemed?" in *Philosophy of Religion: An Anthology,* ed. C. Taliaferro and P. Griffiths (Oxford: Blackwell, 2003), 534–35.

14. Peter van Inwagen, *The Problem of Evil* (Notre Dame: University of Notre Dame Press, 1992); Taliaferro and Griffiths, *Philosophy of Religion: An Anthology*, 396.

15. See Michael Murray, *Nature Red in Tooth and Claw* (Oxford: Oxford University Press, 2008).

16. Van Inwagen, *The Problem of Evil*, 395.

17. Marilyn McCord, "Horrendous Evils and the Goodness of God," in *The Problem of Evil,* ed. Marilyn McCord Adams and Robert Merrihew Adams (Oxford: Oxford University Press, 1990), 220.

18. John Hick, *Evil and the God of Love* (San Francisco: Harper and Row, 1997), 397 (emphasis mine).

19. "Critique by John Hick," in *Encountering Evil,* ed. S. T. Davis (London: Leiden, 2001), 29.

20. D. Cohn-Sherbok, "Jewish Faith and the Holocaust," *Religious Studies* 26 (1990): 292–93.

21. For an excellent treatment of the issues, see Richard Creel, "Divine Impassibility," in *The Blackwell Companion to Philosophy of Religion,* ed. Taliaferro, Draper, and Quinn. I defend passibilism in my *Consciousness and the Mind of God.*

22. Alvin Plantinga, "Self-Profile," in *Alvin Plantinga,* ed. James E. Tomberlin and Peter van Inwagen (Dordrecht: Reidel, 1985), 36.

23. Richard Swinburne, "The Problem of Evil," in *Contemporary Philosophy of Religion*, ed. S. Cahn and D. Shatz (Oxford: Oxford University Press, 1982), 19.

24. Fyodor Dostoyevsky, *The Brothers Karamazov*, trans. Constance Garnett, rev. Ralph E. Matlaw (New York: Norton, 1976), 299.

25. Technically, Schellenberg's argument is aimed at Christian theism and does not support atheism per se. If his argument succeeds, then there may still be a God, just not the God envisioned in Christian tradition.

26. Schellenberg, *The Wisdom to Doubt*, 225.

27. Ibid., 228.

28. A vigorous tradition in Christian spirituality holds that in the soul's journey to God there are times of great aridity and a painful experience of God's withdrawal. Perhaps the greatest student and writer on this process is Saint John of the Cross (1542–1591): "Such souls will likely experience what is called 'the dark night of the soul.' The 'dark night' is when those persons lose all the pleasure that they once experienced in their devotional life. This happens because God wants to purify them and move them on to greater heights." From *The Dark Night of the Soul*, in *Devotional Classics*, ed. R. J. Foster and J. B. Smith (New York: Harper-Collins, 1989), 33. John of the Cross even expresses the sense of God's presence and absence in terms of maternal care: "After a soul has been converted by God, that soul is nurtured and caressed by the Spirit. Like a loving mother, God cares for and comforts the infant soul by feeding it spiritual milk. Such souls will find great delight in this stage. They will begin praying with great urgency and perseverance; they will engage in all kinds of religious activities because of the joy they experience in them. But there will come a time when God will bid them to grow deeper. He will remove the previous consolation from the soul in order to teach it virtue and prevent it from developing vice." Ibid.

29. A. Padgett, "Review of *Divine Hiddenness and Human Reason* by J. L. Schellenberg," *Philosophical Books* 35:3 (1994): 208.

30. Dawkins, *The God Delusion*, 31.

31. François Fénelon, "A Will No Longer Divided," in *Devotional Classics*, ed. Foster and Smith, 52.

32. Dawkins, *The God Delusion*, 108.

33. For an excellent book that replies to many of the moral objections to God in the Bible, see Paul Copan, *Is God a Moral Monster? Making Sense of the Old Testament God* (Grand Rapids: Baker Books, 2011).

34. Richard Swinburne, *The Existence of God* (Oxford: Clarendon Press, 1979), 246.

35. Hick, *The Fifth Dimension*, 23.

36. Hick, *Evil and the God of Love*, 343.

37. Keith Ward, "Sentient Afterlife," in *Animals and Christianity*, ed. A. Linzey and T. Regan (New York: Crossroads, 1988), 104–5.

Chapter 6. Redemption and Time

1. The classical articulation of forgiveness in terms of renouncing resentment can be found in two sermons by Bishop Butler, "Upon Resentment" and "Upon Forgiveness of Injuries," sermons VIII and IX, in *The Works of Joseph Butler*, vol. 2, ed. W. E. Gladstone (Oxford: Clarendon Press), 136–67. For a contemporary position in the tradition of Butler, see Charles Griswold, *Forgiveness: A Philosophical Exploration* (Cambridge: Cambridge University Press, 2007).

2. During the French Revolution, in Dickens's tale, the character Sydney Carton heroically exchanges places with Charles Darnay in prison, thus allowing Charles to escape. Sydney is executed in his place.

3. For an overview of the Christus Victor tradition, see Gustav Aulen, *Christus Victor: A Historical Study of the Three Main Types of the Idea of Atonement*, trans A. G. Hebert (Eugene, OR: Wipf & Stock, 2003).

4. Anselm, "Cur Deus Homo," in *St. Anselm's Basic Writings*, trans. S. N. Deane (Chicago: Open Court, 1998), 192.

5. Another concept in addition to adoption that has been used to capture the saving union (atonement) between God and the soul is that of marriage. As a professor at St. Olaf College (affiliated with the Lutheran tradition), I feel obliged to cite the good Martin Luther on this other metaphor-saving image: "By the wedding ring of faith [Christ] shares in the sins, death, and pains of hell which are his bride's. As a matter of fact, he makes them his own and acts as if they were his own and as if he himself had sinned; he suffered, died, and descended into hell that he might overcome them all. . . . Thus the believing soul by means of the pledge of its faith is free in Christ, its bridegroom . . . and is endowed with the eternal righteousness, life, and salvation of Christ its bridegroom." *Freedom of a Christian,* trans. W. A. Lambert and H. J. Grimm, in *Luther's Works* [American Edition], vol. 31, *Career of the Reformer 1* (Philadelphia: Fortress Press, 1957), 352.

6. Stephen Davis, *Christian Philosophical Theology* (Oxford: Oxford University Press, 2002), 219.

7. Ibid., 221.

8. For further work on Shakespeare and redemption, see my "A Shakespearean Account of Redemption," in *The Psychology of Character and Virtue*, ed. C. S. Titus (Arlington, VA: Institute for the Psychological Sciences, 2008).

9. Clement, "Letter to the Corinthians," in *The Faith of the Early Fathers*, ed. Jurgens, 1:8–9.

10. Cited by John Baillie, *Our Knowledge of God* (London: Oxford University Press, 1963), 18.

11. William Law, *A Serious Call to a Devout and Holy Life*, ed. P. G. Stanwood (New York: Paulist Press, 1978), 395.

12. Philip Quinn, "Abelard on Atonement: Nothing Unintelligible, Arbitrary or Immoral About It," in *Trinity, Incarnation, and Atonement: Philosophical and Theological Essays*, ed. Ronald J. Feenstra and Cornelius Plantinga, Jr. (Notre Dame: University of Notre Dame Press, 1989), 15.

13. Richard Purtill, *Reason to Believe* (San Francisco: Ignatius Press, 2009), 189–90.

14. Irenaeus, "Against Heresies," in *The Faith of the Early Fathers*, ed. Jurgens, 1:87.

15. For an excellent overview of the orthodox affirmation of the goodness of the body over against Gnosticism, see Margaret R. Miles, *Fullness of Life: Historical Foundations for a New Asceticism* (Philadelphia: Westminster Press, 1981).

Chapter 7. Eternity in Time

1. St. Gregory of Elvira, "Homilies on the Books of Sacred Scripture," in *The Faith of Early Fathers*, ed. Jurgens, 1:393.

2. Saint Augustine, *Augustine of Hippo, Selected Writings*, trans. Mary T. Clark (Paulist Press, 1984), 410.

3. Jean Leclercq, O.S.B, *The Love of Learning and the Desire for God*, trans. C. Misrahi (New York: Fordham University Press, 1982), 74.

4. There may also be this difference: if Kris is a four-dimensionalist, then she believes that she is spread out over time. On this view, the whole of Kris cannot be fully present to God at a given moment, but only a part (a time slice) of her life. Still, Kris might rightly claim that the whole of her life (past, present, and future) is present to God insofar as God is present to all creation at all times.

5. Charles Taylor, *A Secular Age* (Cambridge: Harvard University Press, 2007), 55.

6. Ibid., 57.

7. Boethius, *The Consolation of Philosophy* (New York: Random House 1943), 117.

8. Ibid., 81.

9. Augustine, *The City of God*, trans. Marcus Dods (New York: Random House, 1950), 17.

10. Ibid., 3.

11. Leo I, "Sermons," in *The Faith of the Early Fathers*, ed. Jurgens, 2:276.

12. D.M. Baillie, *God Was In Christ* (London: Faber and Faber, 1961), 191.

13. Emil Brunner, *The Mediator* (Philadelphia: Westminster Press, 1947), 504.

14. *Confessions of Saint Augustine*, trans. Pine-Coffin, Book 11, p. 276.

15. Ibid., Book 11, 280.

16. Gregory of Nazianz, "Orations," in *The Faith of the Early Fathers*, ed. Jurgens, 3:38.

17. Bonaventure, *The Soul's Journey to God, The Tree of Life, and The Life of St. Francis*, trans. E. Cousins, Classics of Western Spirituality (New York: Paulist Press, 1978), 171.

18. Gregory of Nyssa, *The Life of Moses*, 2.25.

19. Charles Williams, *Descent into Hell* (Grand Rapids: Eerdmans, 1973), 222.

20. Marlowe Christopher, *Dr. Faustus* (from the Quarto of 1616), 5.4.244–55.

21. Ibid., 5.4.256–63.

22. As an aside, I note that it is not the case that all virtues have this diffuse character. One might love courage, and yet this love is not in itself brave.

23. Kierkegaard, *Works of Love*, 262.

24. D. Z. Phillips, *The Problem of Evil and the Problem of God* (Minneapolis: Fortress Press, 2005), 26.

25. Origen, *Dialogue with Heraclides*, as cited in Margaret R. Miles, *Fullness of Life: Historical Foundations for a New Asceticism* (Philadelphia: Westminster Press, 1981), 47.

26. Johannes Tauler, *Sermons*, trans. M. Shrady (New York: Paulist Press, 1985), 64.

Chapter 8. Glory and the Hallowing of Domestic Virtue

1. G. K. Chesterton, *Collected Works of G. K. Chesterton*, vol. 15, *Chesterton on Dickens*, ed. Alzina Stone Dale (San Francisco: Ignatius Press, 1989), 89.

2. A. E. Taylor, *The Faith of a Moralist* (London: Macmillan, 1951), 110–11.

3. Eric Auerbach, *Mimesis: The Representation of Reality in Western Literature*, trans. W. R. Trask (Princeton: Princeton University Press, 2003), 42–44.

4. Brother Lawrence, from *The Practice of the Presence of God*, in *Devotional Classics*, ed. R. J. Foster and J. B. Smith (New York: HarperOne, 1989), 372–73.

5. Jean Pierre de Caussade, from *The Sacrament of the Present Moment*, in *Devotional Classics*, ed. Foster and Smith, 201.

6. *Sor Juana Inés de la Cruz: Selected Writings*, trans. P. K. Rappaport (New York: Paulist Press, 2005), 274.

7. Coleridge rightly pointed out the Hebrew roots of recognizing the hallowed nature of all creation: "In the Hebrew poets each thing has a life of its own and yet they are all one life. In God they move and live and *have* their being; not *had*, as the cold system of Newtonian Theology represents, but *have*." Coleridge, cited by Auden in *The Complete Works of W. H. Auden; Prose*, ed. E. Mendelson (Princeton: Princeton University Press, 2008), 3:37. See also Thomas Howard, *Splendor in the Ordinary* (Wheaton, IL: Tyndale House, 1977).

8. Dante Alighieri, *La Vita Nuova: Poems of Youth*, trans. Barbara Reynolds (London: Penguin, 1969), 5.

9. Ibid. As a humorous aside, I note that the Dante-Beatrice story provides us a reason why more of us should offer a "sweet greeting" to frustrated writers; the world might have more epic poetry as a result.

10. Dante, *Paradise*, trans. Sayers and Reynolds, 33.144–45 (p. 347).

11. Charles Williams, *The Figure of Beatrice: A Study in Dante* (London: Faber and Faber, 1943), 7–8.

12. For this account and quotation, see http://www.catholic-pages.com/saints/st_maximilian.asp.

13. Ibid.

14. R. S. Thomas, *Laboratories of the Spirit* (Boston: Macmillan, 1975), 60.

15. C. S. Lewis, *Reflections on the Psalms* (New York: Harcourt Brace, 1958), 137–38.

16. See Stephen T. Davis, *Christian Philosophical Theology* (Oxford: Oxford University Press, 2006), especially chap. 4, "Periochoretic Monotheism"; and Richard Swinburne, *The Christian God* (Oxford: Oxford University Press, 1994).

17. Cudworth, "A Sermon Preached before the Honorable House of Commons," in *Cambridge Platonist Spirituality*, ed. Taliaferro and Teply, 92.

18. Clement, "Letter to the Corinthians," in *The Faith of the Early Fathers*, ed. Jurgens, 1:11.

19. Richard of St. Victor, *The Twelve Patriarchs; the Mystical Arts; Book Three of the Trinity*, trans. G. A. Zinn (New York: Paulist Press, 1979), 56–57.

20. John Climacus, *The Ladder of Divine Ascent*, trans. C. Luibheid and N. Russell (New York: Paulist Press, 1982), 228.

INDEX

197

CHARLES TALIAFERRO

is professor of philosophy at St. Olaf College.